1001 Sentence Sermons

Sentence Sermons for Church Signs, Bulletins, Newsletters, Sermons, and Daily Living

L. James Harvey Ph.D.

TRILOGY
PROFESSIONAL PUBLISHING MEETS POWERFUL PROMOTION

A wholly owned subsidiary of TBN

1001 Sentence Sermons

Trilogy Christian Publishers A Wholly Owned Subsidiary of Trinity Broadcasting Network

2442 Michelle Drive Tustin, CA 92780

Copyright © 2021 by L. James Harvey

Published as companion book to *701 Sentence Sermons: Attention-Getting Quotes for Church Signs, Bulletins, Newsletters, and Sermons.* Kregel Publications. 2002

No part of this book may be reproduced, stored in a retrieval system, or transmitted by any means without written permission from the author. All rights reserved. Printed in the USA.

Rights Department, 2442 Michelle Drive, Tustin, CA 92780.

Trilogy Christian Publishing/TBN and colophon are trademarks of Trinity Broadcasting Network.

For information about special discounts for bulk purchases, please contact Trilogy Christian Publishing.

Trilogy Disclaimer: The views and content expressed in this book are those of the author and may not necessarily reflect the views and doctrine of Trilogy Christian Publishing or the Trinity Broadcasting Network.

Manufactured in the United States of America

10 9 8 7 6 5 4 3 2 1

Library of Congress Cataloging-in-Publication Data is available.

ISBN: 978-1-63769-326-1

E-ISBN: 978-1-63769-327-8

Table of Contents

Dedication 5

Book Endorsements 7

Introduction 9

How it Got Started. 11

How to Use this Book 15

Good Suggestions from a Sign Master 17

Advice on Effective Sign Usage. 19

1001 Sentence Sermons. 25

Dedication

I'd like to dedicate this book and the flowers on the cover to Jackie my wonderful wife of 69 years, and best friend. She's also the mother of our four great children Linda, Doug, Leslie, and Lisa.

Let me also here add my thanks to the amazing staff at Trilogy Christian Publishing that has made publishing this book a joy and pleasure.

LJH

Book Endorsements

Each of the earlier volumes have been such a great resource for the fixed letter back lit church sign. Now more recently for our electronic sign! Time is of the essence since drivers must receive the sign message in seconds. These messages have allowed me to accommodate that goal. Cars in our "Drive-by Congregation" number 17,000 per day. I recall two different times different bus drivers told me how they would re-route their school bus in order to be blessed by the message.

Rev. Bill Campbell, member, Oakhill Evangelical Presbyterian Church, Grand Rapids, Michigan

More than two decades ago, Jim Harvey began a sign ministry which immediately catapulted our church's outreach. His sentence sermons made our neighbors smile, laugh, and ponder good news from God. I am delighted to see Jim has mined more nuggets of inspiration and truth in *1001 Sentence Sermons*. I am confident these pithy sayings can do the same thing for your church.

The Rev. Dr. Stephen Nicholas, Pastor 1989-2007, St. Paul's Moravian Church, Upper Marlboro, Maryland

I was blessed to have the opportunity to serve as the Sign Master of our local church for over seven years. Jim's insightful volumes on *Sentence Sermons* were used almost exclusively as the source for the messages. When changing the sign, it was a rewarding experience to receive real time feedback from passing neighbors expressing their appreciation for the messages. Some would even stop and take time to explain how a certain message had personally impacted their lives.

> Merritt "Butch" Aurich, Former Sign Master, St. Paul's Moravian Church, Upper Marlboro, Maryland

Dr. Harvey offers some nifty nuggets of humor and wisdom that will make you howl with laughter (or perhaps cry) but will definitely make you think. Use them to sprinkle your speech, blog, or newsletter with insight and wit.

> Dr. Douglass P. Norwood Jr., Former Executive Director, Broken Jar Ministry, Allentown, Pennsylvania

Having used Jim's previous books of *Sentence Sermons*, I am pleased, with the attention these thought-provoking statements of wit and wisdom have, to invite the public into a mental conversation, if not a personal contact for the church.

> Rev. Thomas Couch, Pastor, Grandville Bible Church, Grandville, Michigan

Introduction

Aphorisms, the academic elite might call them, however, there are many names attached to them. They are called axioms, nuggets, truisms, adages, pearls, proverbs, maxims, dictums, precepts, and sayings. The dictionary defines them as "a concise statement of truth" or "a terse formulation of truth." I prefer to refer to them as "Sentence Sermons" (SSs) because they deal most often with truths that guide our lives. They preach a significant truth we need to pay attention to in order to live a productive life. And in a sense, they often reflect the wisdom of the ages in a concise form.

I have always enjoyed these easily remembered bits of truth, but I paid more attention to them in college and beyond, as I matured in my Christian faith. I tell the story below how I became more deeply involved with them about twenty years ago. I have grown in my appreciation for their potential to change lives and guide people's thinking. I have seen these SSs used on church signs, on commercial sign boards by businesses, in bulletins and newsletters, and even by radio stations as their "thought for the day." Some people start their day by reading one of the SSs from one of the books. I couldn't be more pleased to see how, what started as an experiment by a church in Upper Marlboro, Maryland, has now produced five books of SSs, a web site, and has impacted lives all over the U.S.A. and even overseas.

A commitment to truth is an essential for success in life and is critical to a productive Christian life. These bits of truth can be a blessing to anyone who reads and thinks about them. Read below how this ministry got started and then enjoy some of the fruit it has produced.

How it Got Started

A lady backed her car out of her driveway and headed for highway M37. A busy two-lane road South out of Grand Rapids, Michigan toward Battle Creek. The lady was depressed. Her family was falling a-part. She was facing a divorce. She had decided life was no longer worth living and the best way to end it was to pull in front of a large 18-wheel semi-truck. She reasoned the head-on collision would end her suffering once and for all.

About two years or so before this, in Maryland, a Moravian Church contacted the author to ask him a favor. The church had recently received a gift that allowed them to place a new church sign on the corner of the church property. The corner happened to be a busy four way stop intersection, where many cars passed by each day entering and leaving a large subdivision. The church wanted the author to be responsible for putting messages on the sign containing precious Christian truths. I agreed and immediately called the sign company to find a book or two of sign messages that had been formatted to go on the sign, which had four lines and about twenty spaces per line for letters. The president of the sign company informed me there were no such books in print, and he offered to send me a page or two of some they had. I realized I had a job to do so I began collecting and formatting messages from numerous sources including books of quotes and the Bible. My collection grew over a year or two to a thousand messages, which I labeled "Sentence Sermons."

The depressed lady mentioned above was nearing the town of Middleville, Michigan when she saw a Baptist Church on her right and the church had a sign alongside the road with a message on it. When she read the message, she believed it was meant for her. She pulled into the church parking lot, turned around and went back home. The lady turned her life around and returned to normal. She was thankful for the sign message and wrote a letter to the pastor of the church thanking him for the church sign and the message that had saved her life. The pastor shared the message with his congregation. One of the leaders of the congregation was also the president of a leading Christian publishing company in Grand Rapids, Michigan.

After I had collected 1000 Sentence Sermons and knowing there were no such books on the market with the formatted messages, I began sending manuscripts to various publishers hoping one would publish such a book. I got the usual rejections that authors often get when trying to get a book published. One manuscript, however, hit the desk of the president of the publishing company who was a member of the Baptist church near Middleville. He remembered the lady's letter and reasoned that if a message could save a life maybe these signs were more important than we thought, and a well-developed book of them was needed. The president turned out to be right. The first book published was entitled, *701 Sentence Sermons*. That publishing company went on to publish four volumes of *Sentence Sermons*. The "Sermons" have been

How it Got Started

used all over the U.S.A. as messages on church bulletin boards, in newsletters, on business sign boards, and they have been used by radio stations as their "Thought for the Day." They have led to a Sentence Sermon web site (**www.sentencesermons.com**) and an e-mail list of people wanting new "Sermons" but who did not live near a church using them. Several churches adopted the mindset the author wrote about (a copy is on the web site) that a church should consider the cars passing their church every day as their "drive-by congregation" and their church sign a vehicle for communicating Christian truths to them. Some churches may have two hundred in church on Sunday, but have thousands driving by every day.

When the publisher in Grand Rapids retired that company discontinued the *701 Sentence Sermon* series. However, TBNs Trilogy Publications has picked up the baton and therefore we have an all-new *1001 Sentence Sermon* book.

Our prayer is that these little "Sermons" will find their way into the hearts and minds of people all over the U.S.A. and lead them to a greater understanding of life and of God.

How to Use This Book

Because people's needs, and interpretations may differ, a variety of sentence sermons have been presented in the pages that follow. Some are humorous, some are straight forward, and still others are designed to make people think. Some are from the Bible, some are from Christian thinkers, and others from secular sources that present basic truths. People will react differently to the same sentence sermon depending on their perceptions, theological background, or worldview. If a church, business, organization, or even individuals are to use these sermons publicly, it is important that they be carefully selected to avoid controversy, therefore, a system has been devised and is here presented to carefully select the most valuable use for any group or individual wishing to use them within the copyright limitations offered.

The system presented is a rating system based on a 5-point scale. The system allows for a committee or individual to read the sentence sermons and allows them to rate each one on a 5- point scale with 5 being the highest and best and 1 being the lowest. If a church has a sign master responsible for changing the messages, he or she could then select only messages a committee or the pastor or other individuals have rated a 4 or 5. This would bring the "cream to the top" for that church or organization. The scale is as follows:

1 (Poor)   Do not use
2 (Weak)   Use others
3 (Average) Use 4s and 5s first
4 (Good)   Use 5s first
5 (Best)   Use First

After the sermons have been rated the scores can be tabulated averaged and the potential problems with misunderstood messages avoided. In today's woke society and cancel culture, along with racial and sexual sensitivities, one must be careful what they publish, or put forward, as their views. Until the First Amendment is fully and totally respected by all, everyone needs to be very sensitive and careful.

It is the authors hope and prayer that everyone reading these "Sentence Sermons" will be entertained, enlightened, and finds information and wisdom they'd like to pass on to others.

Good Suggestions from a Sign Master

While finishing the details of this book I received a note from a former Sign Master at St. Paul's Moravian Church where this all got started, as mentioned earlier. Merritt "Butch" Aurich wrote a very compact paragraph of advice for Sign Masters of other churches. I thought I would include it as written and then I'll comment further on how to best use signs today. Because it has a great deal of wisdom packed into a tight paragraph, here's Butch's paragraph:

Thoughts: Keep the messages biblical and away from politics, as well as, relevant to the present times. Only brief soundbites, as most people today seem to be stressed out from work and family dynamics. The best messages are uplifting, encouraging, and hopeful. However, the people need to be reminded or taught that our God is not only a loving Father, but also a just one. Weekly messages should be seasoned (Christmas, Easter etc.). Ensure the physical sign has letters that are easily read from the roadside and that they can be read during both daytime and nighttime hours. It is easier to manage a Sign Ministry staff of no more than two or three members at a time.

Advice for Effective Sign Usage

Let me add some comments, particularly as we seem to have of morphed to a day when electronic signs have become very prevalent. The fixed letter back lighted signs were almost better for a sign ministry than the new exotic electronic signs. The reason is that fixed letter signs with at least 8" letters were usually easier to read and the message was usually up for a full day or more, likely for week or so. Nearly every sign had black letters on a white or light-yellow back lighted background. The contrast between letters and background was as great as you can get. It made it easy on the eye for drivers to focus on the letters and message. I find that churches that have electronic signs with various colors, fonts, and gismos are doing things that make it impossible for passersby to read their messages. We need to remember that most drivers have maybe 4-6 seconds to read a message. So, while electronic signs have some advantages, they also have some disadvantages.

I find some churches now flash several messages one after the other. They even often give the time and temperature to drivers. When they do that, they eliminate the possibility the driver will be able to read a SS. They also list special church events, their web site, list service times, say "Welcome" and who knows what else. Every sign change eliminates a potential sentence sermon message that could be read.

Recently I went by a mega-church near my home. They have two electronic signs about a block apart at two different entrances to the church property. One sign was originally designated for sentence sermons and the other for church announcements, a wonderful way to develop a church sign ministry with a drive-by congregation. I went by to see the message for that day. As I approached the first sign, they had the time and temperature on the sign. I then sped toward the second sign hoping for a message. When I got to it, they had the time and temperature on that one also and it differed slightly from the first one. What a waste! I had the time and temperature on my car's dashboard and didn't need it. People will not go out of their way to go by a church to find out info they don't need. I vowed never to waste my time in the future going by the church because I now cannot depend on getting any spiritual food from them. Most potential drive-by congregants require a consistently dependable message, or they won't bother. Doing what that church did is a good way to kill a drive-by ministry.

I also find churches using exotic fonts where the letters run together and make it difficult for the eye to adjust to the letters and message. When a light color is placed on a light background it makes it more difficult for the eye to define the letters. A church near us with a new sign had a small car crossing the top of their sign one day when I went by. I followed the little car and never read the sign. In short, electronic signs allow us to do marvelous things, but unless they lead to clearer communication with the drive-by

Good Suggestions from a Sign Master

congregation they are counterproductive.

If a church wants to cultivate a drive-by congregation, there are some things that must be done whether you have a fixed letter backlit sign or a new electronic one.

1. It is best if the sign has at least four lines and the capacity for a minimum letter height of 8". A two or three-line sign will work, but messages need to be tailored more carefully to be read fully.

2. Messages must have letters that have as deep a contrast to the background as you can get. Sign masters should pay attention to how experts develop signage on roads for driver safety and instruction. Our road and highway signs are always black letters on white, or white letters on dark green, or black letters on light yellow. There's a reason for that – they are easier to read. Not everyone has 20/20 vision.

3. If a church wants to cultivate a drive-by congregation, the drivers need to know when the sign will have a message and the message must stay up long enough for them to read it. Churches with the new electronic signs must either limit the number of different messages each day or possibly select days when you just do sentence sermons and pile all the other messages on different days, so drivers know for certain they can read a "sermon," not the time and temperature. Nothing frustrates drivers more than to come by a church looking for a Christian truth and find information they don't need, which they usually know already. Just because the software is free that comes with the sign, it need not be used. Fixed letter signs make it

easier to cultivate the drive-bys because they know the sign won't change on them after they read the first line. In short, leave messages up for periods of time allowing drivers to read them.

4. If a church or organization using sentence sermons is at a stop light or a stop sign, they have a real advantage because drivers must slow down or stop giving you a captive audience. This could allow the posting of more than one message or church item depending on how long the light goes before changing and where cars stop in relation to the sign.

5. Use a type of font that has clean letters without fancy additions that make them hard to read.

6. Generally speaking, do not use cursive letters. When letters are joined as in handwriting it makes it harder to read quickly.

7. If you have a two-sided fixed letter sign consider using one side for SSs and one side for church advertisements. If you have an electronic sign, consider using different days for SSs and ads.

8. One last summary point. If a church wants to cultivate a drive-by congregation, the drive-bys need to know when they can go by the church and be *certain* there will be a SS and that it will be presented in the most clear and readable form possible. If a church does this, then you can be certain the messages will be used by the Holy Spirit to impact lives and the church will most likely gain some new members.

One thing I stress for all sign masters is that periodically you drive by your sign at the posted speed limit to get a feel for how long drivers have to read it and what you need to do to make it easier for them. Maybe only very short messages can be used or if you have a captive audience longer ones will work fine. Experiment and learn.

Now on to 1001 Sentence Sermons.

1001 Sentence Sermons

1.   ARROGANCE IS PRIDE IN ACTION IT KILLS CURIOSITY AND LOVE

Rating 1 2 3 4 5 Date Used: _____

2.   A SENSE OF HUMOR IS JUST COMMON SENSE DANCING
— WILLIAM JAMES

Rating 1 2 3 4 5 Date Used: _____

3.   SERVICE TO OTHERS IS LOVE IN ACTION

Rating 1 2 3 4 5 Date Used: _____

4.   DON'T RETIRE, IF YOU DO, YOU'LL NEVER HAVE A DAY OFF

Rating 1 2 3 4 5 Date Used: _____

5. **NOTHING MAKES US SO LONELY AS OUR SECRETS**
    — PAUL TOURNIER

Rating 1 2 3 4 5   Date Used: _____

6. **TALENT WINS GAMES BUT TEAMWORK WINS CHAMPIONSHIPS**
    — MICHAEL JORDAN

Rating 1 2 3 4 5   Date Used: _____

7. **GENIUS IS PERSERVERANCE IN ACTION**
    — MIKE NEWLIN

Rating 1 2 3 4 5   Date Used: _____

8. **YOU AREN'T RICH UNTIL YOU HAVE SOMETHING MONEY CAN'T BUY — G. BROOKS**

Rating 1 2 3 4 5   Date Used: _____

9. **WHEN A PERSON ACTS AGAINST THEIR VALUES, FAILURE FOLLOWS**

Rating 1 2 3 4 5   Date Used: _____

10.   **THE TRUE CHURCH SHOULD EDUCATE SOCIETY NOT BE INFLUENCED BY IT**

Rating   1   2   3   4   5   Date Used: _____

11.   **THE TRUE CHURCH CANNOT BE CONTROLLED BY THE STATE ONLY BY GOD'S TRUTH**

Rating   1   2   3   4   5   Date Used: _____

12.   **KNOWLEDGE SPEAKS BUT WISDON LISTENS**

Rating   1   2   3   4   5   Date Used: _____

13.   **TRUE HUMILITY COMES FROM THINKING MORE ABOUT OTHERS AND LESS ABOUT SELF**

Rating   1   2   3   4   5   Date Used: _____

14.   **MOST TROUBLES IN LIFE COME FROM SAYING YES TOO SOON AND NO TOO LATE**

Rating   1   2   3   4   5   Date Used: _____

15. **TRUE HAPPINESS IN LIFE COMES FROM HAVING GOD'S PEACE AT THE CENTER**

Rating 1 2 3 4 5 Date Used: _____

16. **OUR PATIENCE WILL ACHIEVE MORE THEN OUR FORCE — EDMUND BURKE**

Rating 1 2 3 4 5 Date Used: _____

17. **A MOTHER'S LOVE IS CRITICAL TO THE SUCCESS OF THE HUMAN SPIRIT**

Rating 1 2 3 4 5 Date Used: _____

18. **IF YOU'RE OLD ENOUGH TO KNOW BETTER YOU'RE TO OLD TO DO IT — GEORGE BURNS**

Rating 1 2 3 4 5 Date Used: _____

19. **OUR LIFEGUARD WALKS ON WATER**

Rating 1 2 3 4 5 Date Used: _____

20.   **YOU CAN'T GET GOOD FRUIT WITHOUT SHAKING THE TREE**

Rating   1   2   3   4   5   Date Used: _____

21.   **IF YOU DON'T HAVE THE BREAD OF LIFE YOU'LL BE TOAST**

Rating   1   2   3   4   5   Date Used: _____

22.   **IF YOUR LIFE STINKS YOU NEED A PEW IN CHURCH**

Rating   1   2   3   4   5   Date Used: _____

23.   **TROUBLE SLEEPING? OUR SERMONS MIGHT HELP**

Rating   1   2   3   4   5   Date Used: _____

24.   **IF YOU'RE A SINNER AND DON'T HAVE AC YOU'RE IN BIG TROUBLE**

Rating   1   2   3   4   5   Date Used: _____

25. **COINCIDENCE IS GOD'S WAY OF REMAINING ANONYOMUS**
— ALBERT EINSTEIN

Rating 1 2 3 4 5 Date Used: _____

26. **THE USE OF COMMON SENSE IS A SURPISE TO MOST POLITICIANS**

Rating 1 2 3 4 5 Date Used: _____

27. **BUILD SELF WORTH IN CHRIST NOT NET WORTH IN MAMMON**

Rating 1 2 3 4 5 Date Used: _____

28. **IF GOOD DOES NOT DEFEAT EVIL THEN GOOD IS NOT GOOD**

Rating 1 2 3 4 5 Date Used: _____

29. **GOD NEVER MEASURES OUR SELF-WORTH BY OUR NET WORTH**

Rating 1 2 3 4 5 Date Used: _____

30. LIFE IS THE ART OF
     DRAWING WITHOUT
     AN ERASER
     — JOHN GARDNER

Rating   1   2   3   4   5   Date Used: _____

31. IN A LAND OF
     IMMORALITY GOD
     IS A MORTAL
     ENEMY

Rating   1   2   3   4   5   Date Used: _____

32. WHEN EVERYONE
     SINGS THE SAME
     NOTE THERE IS
     NO HARMONY

Rating   1   2   3   4   5   Date Used: _____

33. LIVE SO NO ONE
     WILL BELIEVE ANY
     ONE WHO SPEAKS
     ILL OF YOU

Rating   1   2   3   4   5   Date Used: _____

34. THERE IS NO VIRTUE
     IN ANY PROMISE
     UNTIL IT IS KEPT

Rating   1   2   3   4   5   Date Used: _____

35. **GOALS SHOULD BE SET TO CAUSE US TO STRETCH A LITTLE**

Rating 1 2 3 4 5 Date Used: _____

36. **THE BEST FACE LIFT IS A SMILE**

Rating 1 2 3 4 5 Date Used: _____

37. **IT IS DESERVING HONORS NOT RECEIVING THEM THAT COUNTS**

Rating 1 2 3 4 5 Date Used: _____

38. **DOLLARS ARE BETTER USED IF ACCOMPANIED BY SENSE**

Rating 1 2 3 4 5 Date Used: _____

39. **INTOLERANCE WITH YOUR PRESENT SITUATION CREATES YOUR FUTURE**

Rating 1 2 3 4 5 Date Used: _____

40. ATTEMPTING TOO MUCH ACCOMPLISHES LITTLE AND DISAPPOINTS MUCH

Rating   1   2   3   4   5   Date Used: _____

41. TO DISAGREE AND STILL HOLD HANDS IS A GIFT

Rating   1   2   3   4   5   Date Used: _____

42. TRUTH DOES NOT CHANGE WITH OUR ABILITY TO STOMACH IT

Rating   1   2   3   4   5   Date Used: _____

43. THE SUNLIGHT OF TRUTH IS THE BEST DISINFECTANT FOR CORRUPT POLITICS

Rating   1   2   3   4   5   Date Used: _____

44. OUR BILL OF RIGHTS ALSO REQUIRES A BILL OF RESPONSIBILITIES

Rating   1   2   3   4   5   Date Used: _____

45. **THE STRONGEST TIMBER GROWS WHERE THE WINDS ARE THE HARSHEST**

Rating 1 2 3 4 5   Date Used: _____

46. **THOSE WHO LIVE BY A CRYSTAL BALL LIVE TO EAT BROKEN GLASS**

Rating 1 2 3 4 5   Date Used: _____

47. **YOU CAN BE OLD AT 30 OR YOUNG AT 80 – IT'S YOUR MIND-SET**

Rating 1 2 3 4 5   Date Used: _____

48. **BE WHO GOD WANTS YOU TO BE NOT WHO OTHERS WANT YOU TO BE**

Rating 1 2 3 4 5   Date Used: _____

49. **THE ESSENCE OF LIFE IS TO KNOW WHO TO LOVE, HOW TO LOVE, AND WHEN TO LOVE**

Rating 1 2 3 4 5   Date Used: _____

50. THE WHOLE OF LIFE IS TO LOVE GOD, OTHERS, AND SELF, AND IN THAT ORDER

Rating 1 2 3 4 5 Date Used: _____

51. NOBILITY WITHOUT VIRTUE IS A FINE SETTING WITHOUT A GEM — JANE PORTER

Rating 1 2 3 4 5 Date Used: _____

52. A NEW BROOM SWEEPS CLEAN BUT AN OLD ONE KNOWS THE CORNERS

Rating 1 2 3 4 5 Date Used: _____

53. APPEASEMENT ON A PRINCIPLE IS DEFEAT ON THE INSTALLMENT PLAN

Rating 1 2 3 4 5 Date Used: _____

54. NEVER LOAN A FRIEND MORE MONEY THAN YOU CAN AFFORD TO LOSE

Rating 1 2 3 4 5 Date Used: _____

55. YOUTH IS NOT A TIME OF LIFE IT IS A STATE OF MIND

Rating 1 2 3 4 5   Date Used: _____

56. THE MORE A PLOUGH IS USED THE BRIGHTER IT SHINES

Rating 1 2 3 4 5   Date Used: _____

57. DEEP ROOTS NEVER DOUBT SPRING WILL COME
— MARTY RUBIN

Rating 1 2 3 4 5   Date Used: _____

58. SINNERS WONDER WHY CHRISTIANS DANCE – IT'S BECAUSE SINNERS CAN'T HEAR THE MUSIC

Rating 1 2 3 4 5   Date Used: _____

59. CHRISTIANS ARE TOO BLESSED TO BE STRESSED

Rating 1 2 3 4 5   Date Used: _____

60. **"GOOD MORNING, THIS IS GOD, I WILL BE HANDLING YOUR PROBLEMS TODAY"**

Rating   1   2   3   4   5   Date Used: _____

61. **LEGISLATED IMMORALITY MOCKS GOD AND INVITES HIS WRATH**

Rating   1   2   3   4   5   Date Used: _____

62. **THE BEST WIRELESS PLAN - PRAYER UNLIMITED DATA UNLIMITED MESSAGES**

Rating   1   2   3   4   5   Date Used: _____

63. **WHEN YOUR TRAIN OF THOUGHT LEAVES THE STATION BE SURE YOU'RE ON IT**

Rating   1   2   3   4   5   Date Used: _____

64. **THE U.S.A. IS THE HOME OF THE FREE BECAUSE OF THE BRAVE**

Rating   1   2   3   4   5   Date Used: _____

65. SARCASM IS THE MIND'S NATURAL DEFENSE AGAINST STUPIDITY

Rating 1 2 3 4 5   Date Used: _____

66. GIVING JOY TO OTHERS CAUSES IT TO RETURN TO THE GIVER IN INCREASING MEASURE

Rating 1 2 3 4 5   Date Used: _____

67. WHEN THINGS GO BAD DON'T GO WITH THEM

Rating 1 2 3 4 5   Date Used: _____

68. AT CHRISTMAS ALL ROADS LEAD HOME — M. HOLMES

Rating 1 2 3 4 5   Date Used: _____

69. CHRISTMAS WAS THE BEGINNING OF THE END OF EVIL

Rating 1 2 3 4 5   Date Used: _____

70. A CHILD OF THE KING SHOULD BEAR A FAMILY RESEMBLANCE

Rating 1 2 3 4 5 Date Used: _____

71. DIVERSITY IS PERVERSITY IF IT MINIMIZES CHRIST'S BIRTH OR SACRIFICE

Rating 1 2 3 4 5 Date Used: _____

72. GOD IS BOTH AMERICA'S GREATEST HOPE AND GREATEST THREAT — DR. ADRIAN ROGERS

Rating 1 2 3 4 5 Date Used: _____

73. CHRISTIANS DO NOT LOSE UNTIL THEY QUIT

Rating 1 2 3 4 5 Date Used: _____

74. IF YOU SMILE WHEN YOU ARE ALONE YOU'RE REALLY HAPPY

Rating 1 2 3 4 5 Date Used: _____

75. **THE ILLUSION OF KNOWLEDGE IS THE GREATEST HINDRINCE TO PROGRESS**

Rating   1   2   3   4   5   Date Used: _____

76. **LOOK AT LIFE THRU THE WINDSHIELD NOT THE REAR VIEW MIRROR - B. BAGGETT**

Rating   1   2   3   4   5   Date Used: _____

77. **KEEP YOUR HEAD UP ALWAYS BUT NOT YOUR NOSE**

Rating   1   2   3   4   5   Date Used: _____

78. **COUNT YOUR BLESSINGS BUT NOT BIRTHDAYS**

Rating   1   2   3   4   5   Date Used: _____

79. **FRAUD AND DECIET PREFER THE DARK TRUTH LOVES THE LIGHT**

Rating   1   2   3   4   5   Date Used: _____

80. WE CAN'T CHANGE THE WIND BUT WE CAN ADJUST OUR SAILS

Rating 1 2 3 4 5 Date Used: _____

81. WORRY DOES NOT REMOVE TROUBLE BUT IT DOES REMOVE PEACE

Rating 1 2 3 4 5 Date Used: _____

82. SOMETIMES THE EMOTIONS SEE WHAT EYE CANNOT SEE

Rating 1 2 3 4 5 Date Used: _____

83. NO WIND IS FAVORABLE TO THE SAILOR WHO HAS NO COMPASS

Rating 1 2 3 4 5 Date Used: _____

84. LET YOUR HEART FEEL FOR THE AFFLICTION AND DISTRESS OF EVERYONE — GEORGE WASHINTON

Rating 1 2 3 4 5 Date Used: _____

85. **WE MAY BE OLD IN YEARS, BUT WE CAN STILL SEE EACH DAY AS WONDERFULLY NEW**

Rating   1   2   3   4   5   Date Used: _____

86. **IF YOU HAVE BROKEN THE EGGS YOU SHOULD MAKE THE OMELET — ANTHONY EDEN**

Rating   1   2   3   4   5   Date Used: _____

87. **LISTENING CAREFULLY TO OTHERS MAY BE THE SINCEREST ACT OF AFFECTION**

Rating   1   2   3   4   5   Date Used: _____

88. **A GOOD LAUGH AND A GOOD NIGHTS SLEEP WILL CURE MOST ILLS**

Rating   1   2   3   4   5   Date Used: _____

89. **CONCEALING WOUNDS THAT HAVE NOT HEALED IS NOT WISE**

Rating   1   2   3   4   5   Date Used: _____

90. YOUR BRAIN HAS ITS
OWN POWER SOURCE
DON'T WAIT TO
GET PLUGGED IN

Rating 1 2 3 4 5 Date Used: _____

91. SOMETIMES GOD LETS
US HIT ROCK BOTTOM
SO WE'LL FIND OUT HE'S THE
ROCK AT THE BOTTOM

Rating 1 2 3 4 5 Date Used: _____

92. TRUE HUMILITY
INVOLVES MAKING A
CORRECT ESTIMATE
OF ONES SELF

Rating 1 2 3 4 5 Date Used: _____

93. IF YOU LOVE OTHERS
THEY WILL WANT TO
HANG OUT WITH YOU

Rating 1 2 3 4 5 Date Used: _____

94. WHEN WE LOOK AT
THE SON THRU TEARS
WE CAN SEE A
BEAUTIFUL RAINBOW

Rating 1 2 3 4 5 Date Used: _____

95. FOOLS LIVE TO REGRET THEIR WORDS, WISE MEN REGRET THEIR SILENCE — W. HENRY

Rating 1 2 3 4 5 Date Used: _____

96. SYMPATHY IS A LITTLE MEDICINE TO SOOTHE THE ACHE IN ANOTHERS HEART

Rating 1 2 3 4 5 Date Used: _____

97. WANT A HOME IMPROVEMENT IDEA? TAKE YOUR FAMILY TO CHURCH

Rating 1 2 3 4 5 Date Used: _____

98. JESUS DIDN'T SET US FREE TO SIN HE SET US FREE FROM SIN

Rating 1 2 3 4 5 Date Used: _____

99. SIN WILL LOVE YOU FOR A SEASON AND CURSE YOU FOR ETERNITY

Rating 1 2 3 4 5 Date Used: _____

100. RELIGION IS HANGING AROUND THE CROSS CHRISTIANITY IS GETTING ON THE CROSS

Rating 1 2 3 4 5   Date Used: _____

101. LOVE LETS OTHERS BE THEMSELVES NOT WHO WE WANT THEM TO BE

Rating 1 2 3 4 5   Date Used: _____

102. FALLING IN THE WATER DOESN'T CAUSE DROWNING STAYING UNDER DOES

Rating 1 2 3 4 5   Date Used: _____

103. SPEND YOUR TIME WELL – YOU CAN'T TAKE IT WITH YOU

Rating 1 2 3 4 5   Date Used: _____

104. THE EARLY BIRD GETS THE WORM BUT THE SECOND MOUSE GETS THE CHEESE

Rating 1 2 3 4 5   Date Used: _____

105. ONE CHILD MAKES YOU A PARENT TWO MAKE YOU A REFEREE

Rating 1 2 3 4 5   Date Used: _____

106. WISDOM CREATES CHARACTER

Rating 1 2 3 4 5   Date Used: _____

107. WE DON'T GET TO VOTE ON WHAT GOD ACTUALLY BELIEVES

Rating 1 2 3 4 5   Date Used: _____

108. WITH MORALITY LAWS ARE UNNECESSARY WITHOUT IT LAWS ARE UNENFORCEABLE

Rating 1 2 3 4 5   Date Used: _____

109. WE ALWAYS DO BETTER THAT WHICH WE ENJOY DOING AND ARE GIFTED TO DO

Rating 1 2 3 4 5   Date Used: _____

110.   **HARMONY MAKES IDEAS GROW, LACK OF IT KILLS PROGRESS**

Rating   1   2   3   4   5   Date Used: _____

111.   **VIRTUE IS NOT VIRTUE IF IT IS NOT CONSISTENT**

Rating   1   2   3   4   5   Date Used: _____

112.   **TACT IS THE ABILITY TO SEE OTHERS AS THEY WISH TO BE SEEN**

Rating   1   2   3   4   5   Date Used: _____

113.   **FORGIVING DOESN'T CHANGE THE PAST BUT IT DOES CHANGE THE FUTURE**

Rating   1   2   3   4   5   Date Used: _____

114.   **APOLOGIES ARE THE SUPER GLUE OF LIFE**

Rating   1   2   3   4   5   Date Used: _____

115. HONEST DISAGREEMENT
CAN ONLY OCCUR IN
A STRONG RELATIONSHIP
AND MAKE IT BETTER

Rating 1 2 3 4 5 Date Used: _____

116. TRY NEW THINGS
REMEMBER AMATEURS
BUILT THE ARK
EXPERTS THE TITANIC

Rating 1 2 3 4 5 Date Used: _____

117. THEY WHO SACRIFICE
CONSCIENCE FOR
AMBITION COMMIT
SPIRITUAL SUICIDE

Rating 1 2 3 4 5 Date Used: _____

118. DISCIPLINE ALWAYS
COSTS LESS THAN
THE PRICE OF REGRET

Rating 1 2 3 4 5 Date Used: _____

119. JOY IS A CHOICE
NOT AN OUTCOME
— BETH JOHNSON

Rating 1 2 3 4 5 Date Used: _____

120. A WARM HEART IS BETTER THAN A HOT HEAD

Rating   1   2   3   4   5   Date Used: _____

121. GOOGLE CAN'T ANSWER LIFE'S MOST IMPORTANT QUESTIONS

Rating   1   2   3   4   5   Date Used: _____

122. TO BE ALMOST SAVED IS TO BE TOTALLY LOST

Rating   1   2   3   4   5   Date Used: _____

123. OUR HOLY WATER HAS HAD THE HELL BOILED OUT OF IT

Rating   1   2   3   4   5   Date Used: _____

124. IF YOU PARTY IN HELL YOU'LL BE THE BARBEQUE

Rating   1   2   3   4   5   Date Used: _____

125. GRACE DOES NOT MAKE GOD MORE TOLERANT OF SIN

Rating   1   2   3   4   5   Date Used: _____

126. WHEN FEAR KNOCKS LET FAITH ANSWER THE DOOR

Rating   1   2   3   4   5   Date Used: _____

127. IF A NATION THAT IS IGNORANT AND GODLESS EXPECTS TO BE FREE THEY ARE TRULY STUPID

Rating   1   2   3   4   5   Date Used: _____

128. THE REAL SEPARATION OF CHURCH AND STATE WILL BE THE RAPTURE

Rating   1   2   3   4   5   Date Used: _____

129. A KIND WORD IS LIKE A SPRING DAY
— RUSSIAN PROVERB

Rating   1   2   3   4   5   Date Used: _____

130. A PRINCIPLED PERSON IS ONE WITH A PASSION FOR TRUTH AND RIGHTEOUSNESS

Rating 1 2 3 4 5 Date Used: _____

131. TEMPER BRINGS OUT THE BEST IN STEEL AND THE WORST IN PEOPLE

Rating 1 2 3 4 5 Date Used: _____

132. IT IS BETTER TO GIVE THAN TO LEND AND IT COSTS ABOUT THE SAME — P. GIBBS

Rating 1 2 3 4 5 Date Used: _____

133. GREATNESS IS A LOT SMALL THINGS DONE WELL, EVERY DAY — LEWIS HOWES

Rating 1 2 3 4 5 Date Used: _____

134. LOOK FOR THE BEST IN PEOPLE USE A MAGNIFYING GLASS IF NECESSARY

Rating 1 2 3 4 5 Date Used: _____

135. DEMOCRACY CAN NOT LONG EXIST WITHOUT A MORAL FOUNDATION

Rating 1 2 3 4 5 Date Used: _____

136. A DEMOCRACY WITHOUT A GOD BASED MORALITY IS A ROPE OF SAND

Rating 1 2 3 4 5 Date Used

137. NO GOVERNMENT IS SO PERFECTLY DESIGNED AS TO MAKE VIRTUE AND FAITH UNNECESSARY

Rating 1 2 3 4 5 Date Used: _____

138. MANS' ATTEMPT TO BECOME GOD RESULTS IN THE DYING OF SOULS

Rating 1 2 3 4 5 Date Used: _____

139. NO SUCCESSFUL CIVILIZATION IN HISTORY HAS EVER BEEN BUILT ON ATHEISM

Rating 1 2 3 4 5 Date Used: _____

140. **GRATITUDE IS THE SIGN OF A NOBLE SPIRIT**

Rating 1 2 3 4 5 Date Used: _____

141. **COURTESY IS VERY CONTAGEOUS - START AN EPIDEMIC**

Rating 1 2 3 4 5 Date Used: _____

142. **LUKEWARMNESS NEVER GETS HOT ENOUGH TO COOK THE SIN OUT**

Rating 1 2 3 4 5 Date Used: _____

143. **BIG PROBLEMS OFTEN DISGUISE HIDDEN OPPORTUNITIES**

Rating 1 2 3 4 5 Date Used: _____

144. **THE FRIENDS OF OUR FRIENDS ARE OUR FRIENDS — AFRICAN PROVERB**

Rating 1 2 3 4 5 Date Used: _____

145. **FALL IS THE TIME GOD RELEASES A MASTERPIECE OF BEAUTY IN NATURE**

Rating 1 2 3 4 5 Date Used: _____

146. **LAUGHTER INVOLVES SMALL MUSCLES LIFTING LARGE BURDENS**

Rating 1 2 3 4 5 Date Used: _____

147. **AGING IS HELPFUL - DIMINISHING ENERGY MAKES IT HARDER TO SIN**

Rating 1 2 3 4 5 Date Used: _____

148. **A MISTAKE GRACEFULLY ADMITTED IS A VICTORY**

Rating 1 2 3 4 5 Date Used: _____

149. **SOME PEOPLE ARE SO POOR THAT ALL THEY HAVE IS MONEY**

Rating 1 2 3 4 5 Date Used: _____

150. A PERSON CAN'T STAY GROUNDED UNLESS THEY ARE LOOKING UP

Rating 1 2 3 4 5   Date Used: _____

151. ENJOYING HARD WORK IS NOT ONLY COMPATIBLE BUT ESSENTIAL TO SUCCESS

Rating 1 2 3 4 5   Date Used: _____

152. DON'T JUST COUNT YOUR BLESSINGS MAKE YOUR BLESSINGS COUNT

Rating 1 2 3 4 5   Date Used: _____

153. PLANT LOVE WHERE THERE IS NONE AND WATCH IT GROW

Rating 1 2 3 4 5   Date Used: _____

154. TOO MUCH INFORMATION CAN DESTROY COMMON SENSE

Rating 1 2 3 4 5   Date Used: _____

155. **IF YOU DON'T MANAGE YOUR POSSESSIONS WELL THEY WILL MANAGE YOU**

Rating 1 2 3 4 5 Date Used: _____

156. **IF YOU DON'T TELL THE TRUTH SOMEONE ELSE WILL**

Rating 1 2 3 4 5 Date Used: _____

157. **DON'T KICK THE BUCKET UNTIL YOU'RE SURE IT IS EMPTY**

Rating 1 2 3 4 5 Date Used: _____

158. **WISDOM, UNLIKE GOLD, IS A TREASURE THAT GAINS VALUE WHEN IT IS SPENT**

Rating 1 2 3 4 5 Date Used: _____

159. **WE NEED NOT THINK ALIKE TO LOVE ALIKE
— FRANCIS DAVID**

Rating 1 2 3 4 5 Date Used: _____

160. **FAITH MAKES THINGS POSSIBLE NOT EASY**

Rating   1   2   3   4   5   Date Used: _____

161. **LENT IS SPRING TRAINING FOR CHRISTIANS**

Rating   1   2   3   4   5   Date Used: _____

162. **EVERY SAINT HAS A PAST – EVERY SINNER HAS A FUTURE**

Rating   1   2   3   4   5   Date Used: _____

163. **PRAY FOR HIS REIGN**

Rating   1   2   3   4   5   Date Used: _____

164. **A PERSON IS KNOWN FOR THE COMPANY THEY AVOID**

Rating   1   2   3   4   5   Date Used: _____

165. **EASTER IS MORE THAN SOMETHING TO DYE FOR**

Rating   1   2   3   4   5   Date Used: _____

166. IT IS ALWAYS SPRINGTIME IN THE HEART THAT LOVES GOD

Rating 1 2 3 4 5 Date Used: _____

167. PESSIMISTS NEED A KICK IN THE CAN'TS

Rating 1 2 3 4 5 Date Used: _____

168. IN GOD'S GARDEN: LETTUCE BE KIND SQUASH GOSSIP BEET EVIL

Rating 1 2 3 4 5 Date Used: _____

169. PREPARE FOR YOUR FINALS – STUDY YOUR BIBLE

Rating 1 2 3 4 5 Date Used: _____

170. LET NO ONE EVER COME TO YOU WITHOUT LEAVING HAPPIER AND BETTER

Rating 1 2 3 4 5 Date Used: _____

171. OUR CONGREGATION IS LIKE FUDGE MOSTLY SWEET WITH A FEW NUTS

Rating 1 2 3 4 5   Date Used: _____

172. DON'T CONDONE WHAT GOD CONDEMNS

Rating 1 2 3 4 5   Date Used: _____

173. WHEN THE LAST TRUMPET SOUNDS WE'RE OUTTA HERE

Rating 1 2 3 4 5   Date Used: _____

174. ALWAYS PUT OFF UNTIL TOMORROW WHAT YOU SHOULD NOT DO AT ALL

Rating 1 2 3 4 5   Date Used: _____

175. PRAYER IS SPIRITUAL EXERCISE – ARE YOU IN SHAPE?

Rating 1 2 3 4 5   Date Used: _____

176. **OUR KEY TO HEAVEN WAS HUNG ON A NAIL**

Rating 1 2 3 4 5 Date Used: _____

177. **FOR THE ROAD TO HEAVEN TURN RIGHT AND GO STRAIGHT**

Rating 1 2 3 4 5 Date Used: _____

178. **BIRDS HAVE BILLS TOO BUT THEY KEEP ON SINGING**

Rating 1 2 3 4 5 Date Used: _____

179. **WHAT THE CATERPILLAR SEES AS THE END GOD SEES A BUTTERFLY**

Rating 1 2 3 4 5 Date Used: _____

180. **PATIENCE IS THE COMPANION OF WISDOM — ST. AUGUSTINE**

Rating 1 2 3 4 5 Date Used: _____

181. JESUS CAME ON CHRISTMAS AND ROSE ON EASTER MISSION ACCOMPLISHED

Rating 1 2 3 4 5   Date Used: _____

182. ANGER IS THE ONLY THING WE SHOULD PUT OFF UNTIL TOMORROW

Rating 1 2 3 4 5   Date Used: _____

183. IF THE GOING IS TOO EASY WATCHOUT YOU MAY BE GOING DOWNHILL

Rating 1 2 3 4 5   Date Used: _____

184. EXERCISE EARLY IN MORNING BEFORE YOUR BRAIN FIGURES OUT WHAT YOU'RE DOING

Rating 1 2 3 4 5   Date Used: _____

185. WHEN GREED EXCEEDS NEED, HAPPINESS AND JOY RECEED

Rating 1 2 3 4 5   Date Used: _____

186. NO ROAD IS LONG
WITH GOOD
COMPANY
— TURKISH PROVERB

Rating 1 2 3 4 5   Date Used: _____

187. FOOLS LOOK TO
TOMORROW; WISE
MEN USE TONIGHT
— SCOTTISH PROVERB

Rating 1 2 3 4 5   Date Used: _____

188. A STRONG SENSE OF
SELF AND GOD ARE
ESSENTIAL FOR TRUE
HUMILITY

Rating 1 2 3 4 5   Date Used: _____

189. TRUE COMPASSION
DETHRONES SELF
AND EMPOWERS
LOVE

Rating 1 2 3 4 5   Date Used: _____

190. TO PRETEND WE DON'T
NEED LOVE IS STUPID
AND SELF DEFEATING

Rating 1 2 3 4 5   Date Used: _____

191. SELFISHNESS AND GREED CAUSE MOST OF OUR TROUBLES

Rating 1 2 3 4 5   Date Used: _____

192. CHARACTER IS THE ONLY SECURE FOUNDATION OF THE STATE
— CALVIN COOLIDGE

Rating 1 2 3 4 5   Date Used: _____

193. WHEN KNOWLEDGE SPEAKS WISDOM LISTENS

Rating 1 2 3 4 5   Date Used: _____

194. A DAY IS MADE SUPERB WHEN TOUCHED BY KINDNESS

Rating 1 2 3 4 5   Date Used: _____

195. IF YOU GET GIVE IF YOU LEARN TEACH

Rating 1 2 3 4 5   Date Used: _____

196. THERE ARE NO SHORT CUTS TO HEAVEN THERE'S ONLY JESUS

Rating 1 2 3 4 5   Date Used: _____

197. **TRUE LOVE IS FOUND IN GENEROUS DEEDS DONE SILENTLY**

Rating 1 2 3 4 5 Date Used: _____

198. **THE SWEETEST REVENGE IS TO FORGIVE**
— ISSAC FRIEDMAN

Rating 1 2 3 4 5 Date Used: _____

199. **THAT IS NOT RIGHT ARE THE WORDS OF TRUE PATRIOTS**

Rating 1 2 3 4 5 Date Used: _____

200. **A PRETTY FACE IS NOTHING IF ONE HAS AN UGLY HEART**

Rating 1 2 3 4 5 Date Used: _____

201. **GREAT MUSIC IS WHAT GOOD FEELINGS SOUND LIKE**

Rating 1 2 3 4 5 Date Used: _____

202. **CONSCIOUSLY LETTING GO OF SADNESS IS WHAT CAN MAKE US HAPPY**

Rating 1 2 3 4 5 Date Used: _____

203. WE ARE NOT HUMANS BEING SPIRITUAL WE ARE SPIRITUAL BEINGS IN A HUMAN EXPERIENCE

Rating 1 2 3 4 5   Date Used: _____

204. IT IS BETTER TO WALK ALONE THAN WITH A COMPANY GOING THE WRONG WAY

Rating 1 2 3 4 5   Date Used: _____

205. NO WATER IS TOO DEEP IF YOU KNOW HOW TO SWIM

Rating 1 2 3 4 5   Date Used: _____

206. FAILURE IS ONLY POSTPONED SUCCESS IF ONE PERSISTS

Rating 1 2 3 4 5   Date Used: _____

207. LEARNING TO SAY NO WILL BE OF MORE VALUE THAN LEARNING LATIN — C. SPURGEON

Rating 1 2 3 4 5   Date Used: _____

208. **IF YOU SHAKE THE TREE STAY TO PICK UP THE FRUIT**

Rating   1   2   3   4   5   Date Used: _____

209. **OUR HOPE AND SALVATION ARE IN HEAVEN NOT WASHINGTON D.C.**

Rating   1   2   3   4   5   Date Used: _____

210. **NO BURDEN IS TOO HEAVY TO CARRY WHEN GOD IS HELPING US CARRY IT**

Rating   1   2   3   4   5   Date Used: _____

211. **YOU AND GOD ARE A MAJORITY**

Rating   1   2   3   4   5   Date Used: _____

212. **A MOTHER'S LOVE IS PEACE PERSONIFIED**

Rating   1   2   3   4   5   Date Used: _____

213. **RUNNING THE RACE IS EASY IT'S THE PREPARATION THAT'S HARD**

Rating   1   2   3   4   5   Date Used: _____

214. REST DOES THE LAZY MAN NO GOOD

Rating 1 2 3 4 5   Date Used: _____

215. MINDS ARE LIKE FLOWERS THEY ABSORB THE SUN ONLY WHEN OPEN

Rating 1 2 3 4 5   Date Used: _____

216. THE GREATEST FOE OF SUCCESS IS IN GETTING TOO COMFORTABLE

Rating 1 2 3 4 5   Date Used: _____

217. THERE'S A FINE LINE BETWEEN GENIUS AND INSANITY ERASE IT

Rating 1 2 3 4 5   Date Used: _____

218. PEOPLE SAY NOTHING IS IMPOSSIBLE BUT SOME PEOPLE DO NOTHING EVERY DAY

Rating 1 2 3 4 5   Date Used: _____

219. IF THOU CANST NOT
SEE THE BOTTOM
DON'T WADE
— ENGLISH PROVERB

Rating 1 2 3 4 5   Date Used: _____

220. FAILURE BORN OF
CONVICTION IS
TOLERABLE

Rating 1 2 3 4 5   Date Used: _____

221. A TRUE CHRISTIAN
JOY REACHES
OUR FACES

Rating 1 2 3 4 5   Date Used: _____

222. PRAYER IS A TIME TO
ENJOY A CLOSENESS
WITH OUR HEAVENLY
FATHER

Rating 1 2 3 4 5   Date Used: _____

223. IT IS A CHRISTIAN
DUTY TO BE AS
HAPPY AS WE CAN
BE — C.S. LEWIS

Rating 1 2 3 4 5   Date Used: _____

224. NECESSITY NEVER MADE A GOOD BARGAIN
— BEN FRANKLIN

Rating   1   2   3   4   5   Date Used: _____

225. IF THE PAST DOESN'T TEACH THE PRESENT BOTH LOSE

Rating   1   2   3   4   5   Date Used: _____

226. IRRITATIONS CAUSE PEARLS AND HUMAN PROGRESS

Rating   1   2   3   4   5   Date Used: _____

227. A CHIP ON THE SHOULDER IS BEST DISLODGED BY A PAT ON THE BACK

Rating   1   2   3   4   5   Date Used: _____

228. LIFE IS THE SUM OF YOUR CHOICES
— ALBERT CAMUS

Rating   1   2   3   4   5   Date Used: _____

229. **SERVING GOD MAY REQUIRE LEAVING OUR COMFORT ZONE**

Rating   1   2   3   4   5   Date Used: _____

230. **A CARELESS WORD MAY CAUSE A WOUND THAT TAKES YEARS TO HEAL**

Rating   1   2   3   4   5   Date Used: _____

231. **NEVER COUNT THE TIMES YOU FORGIVE GOD KEEPS SCORE**

Rating   1   2   3   4   5   Date Used: _____

232. **YOU CAN'T BE MISERABLE IF YOU ARE ACTIVELY DOING SOMETHING GOOD**

Rating   1   2   3   4   5   Date Used: _____

233. **THE MORNING IS WISER THAN THE EVENING — RUSSIAN PROVERB**

Rating   1   2   3   4   5   Date Used: _____

234. CALMNESS OF THE MIND IS ONE OF THE SPOT ON BLESSINGS OF TRUE FAITH

Rating 1 2 3 4 5 Date Used: _____

235. HONESTY ABOUT OUR SELFISHNESS IS THE KEY TO LOVING RELATIONSHIPS

Rating 1 2 3 4 5 Date Used: _____

236. TRUE HAPPINESS RESIDES IN OUR ABILITY TO LOVE GOD AND OTHERS

Rating 1 2 3 4 5 Date Used: _____

237. NO, CLOSES DOORS YES, OPENS THEM

Rating 1 2 3 4 5 Date Used: _____

238. FUEL ALONE WILL NOT LIGHT A FIRE
— CHINESE PROVERB

Rating 1 2 3 4 5 Date Used: _____

239. **ADMITTING WE'RE WRONG IS ANOTHER WAY OF SAYING WE ARE NOW WISER**

Rating 1 2 3 4 5 Date Used: _____

240. **FEAR IS OFTEN A ROADBLOCK TO SUCCESS**

Rating 1 2 3 4 5 Date Used: _____

241. **LEARN TO HOLD LOOSLEY ALL THAT IS NOT ETERNAL — MAUDE ROYDEN**

Rating 1 2 3 4 5 Date Used: _____

242. **TO BE SUCCESSFUL YOU MUST LEARN TO HANDLE FAILURE**

Rating 1 2 3 4 5 Date Used: _____

243. **POLITICIANS ARE LIKE DIAPERS THEY NEED TO BE CHANGED OFTEN AND FOR THE SAME REASON — PAUL HARVEY**

Rating 1 2 3 4 5 Date Used: _____

244. LOVE, TRUTH, PEACE, AND JOY ARE THE BEST ELIXIRS IN THE UNIVERSE

Rating 1 2 3 4 5 Date Used: _____

245. NEVER FEAR SHADOWS THEY MEANS THERE'S A LIGHT SOMEWHERE

Rating 1 2 3 4 5 Date Used: _____

250. TO ACHIEVE GREATNESS STOP ASKING PERMISSION

Rating 1 2 3 4 5 Date Used: _____

251. THE GOOD AND THE WISE LEAD QUIET LIVES

Rating 1 2 3 4 5 Date Used: _____

252. YOU DON'T HAVE A LEG TO STAND ON IF THEY ARE BOTH IN YOUR MOUTH

Rating 1 2 3 4 5 Date Used: _____

253. SOME DAYS YOU ARE THE PIGEON AND SOME DAYS THE STATUE

Rating 1 2 3 4 5   Date Used: _____

254. DON'T BURN YOUR BRIDGE WHILE STANDING ON IT

Rating 1 2 3 4 5   Date Used: _____

255. CHRISTIANS ARE IN TRAINING FOR REIGNING

Rating 1 2 3 4 5   Date Used: _____

256. AMERICA WILL LAST ONLY AS LONG AS WE ARE A PEOPLE OF VIRTUE

Rating 1 2 3 4 5   Date Used: _____

257. CHARACTER IS FORGED IN SILENCE AND REVEALED IN CRISIS

Rating 1 2 3 4 5   Date Used: _____

258. NEVER SUSTITUTE
PRAYER FOR
OBEDIENCE

Rating   1   2   3   4   5   Date Used: _____

259. FEAR IS ONLY AS
DEEP AS THE
MIND ALLOWS
— JAPANESE PROVERB

Rating   1   2   3   4   5   Date Used: _____

260. HEARING WHAT ISN'T
SAID IS CRITICAL IN
GOOD COMMUNICATION
— PETER DRUCKER

Rating   1   2   3   4   5   Date Used: _____

261. USE YOUR BRAIN TO
FIND THE FACTS –
USE YOUR HEART
TO FACE THEM

Rating   1   2   3   4   5   Date Used: _____

262. OUR JOB IS TO BRING
JESUS TO THEM AND
LET THE SPIRIT BRING
THEM TO HIM

Rating   1   2   3   4   5   Date Used: _____

263. **A PERSON CAN'T STAY GROUNDED UNLESS THEY ARE LOOKING UP**

Rating   1   2   3   4   5   Date Used: _____

264. **PICK YOUR FRIENDS BUT NOT TO PIECES**

Rating   1   2   3   4   5   Date Used: _____

265. **SERVING OTHERS PROVIDES HEALTH, HAPPINESS, AND LONG LIFE**

Rating   1   2   3   4   5   Date Used: _____

266. **SOMETIMES A GOOD FALL WILL HELP US LEARN WHERE WE TRULY STAND**

Rating   1   2   3   4   5   Date Used: _____

267. **STRAIGHTEN OUT THE PRESENT AND THE FUTURE WILL FALL IN LINE**

Rating   1   2   3   4   5   Date Used: _____

268. THE ONLY FEAR
WORTH HAVING
IS OF GOD

Rating 1 2 3 4 5 Date Used: _____

269. HAPPINES, FREEDOM,
AND PEACE ARE BEST
BEST ATTAINED BY GIVING
THEM TO OTHERS

Rating 1 2 3 4 5 Date Used: _____

270. PRAY AS IF ALL
DEPENDED ON GOD
WORK AS IF ALL
DEPENDED ON YOU

Rating 1 2 3 4 5 Date Used: _____

271. DELAY IS THE
DEADLIEST FORM
OF DENIAL
— J. N. PARKINSON

Rating 1 2 3 4 5 Date Used: _____

272. IF YOU DON'T LEARN
FROM YOUR
MISTAKES WHY
MAKE THEM?

Rating 1 2 3 4 5 Date Used: _____

273. **EVERYONE LOVES
A GOOD LISTENER**

Rating   1   2   3   4   5   Date Used: _____

274. **LOVE BEGETS
EMPATHY WHICH
BEGETS FRIENDSHIP**

Rating   1   2   3   4   5   Date Used: _____

275. **FRIENDSHIP IS GOD'S
WAY OF LOVING US
THROUGH SOMEONE ELSE**

Rating   1   2   3   4   5   Date Used: _____

276. **PROPHESY CLASS
CANCELLED DUE TO
UNFORSEEN
CIRCUMSTANCES**

Rating   1   2   3   4   5   Date Used: _____

277. **DON'T FEAR DOUBT
IT CAN LEAD
TO TRUTH**

Rating   1   2   3   4   5   Date Used: _____

278. **A WISE PERSON PROPORTIONS THEIR BELIEFS TO THE EVIDENCE**

Rating 1 2 3 4 5 Date Used: _____

279. **DON'T BEAR TROUBLE USE IT – TURN IT INTO A TESTIMONY**

Rating 1 2 3 4 5 Date Used: _____

280. **ONE OF SCRIPTURE'S STRENGTHS IS IN ITS ESSENTIAL UNITY**

Rating 1 2 3 4 5 Date Used: _____

281. **SOME PEOPLE DON'T BELIEVE IN GOD BUT THEY HATE HIM ANYWAY**

Rating 1 2 3 4 5 Date Used: _____

282. **SOME PEOPLE DON'T BELIEVE IN GOD BUT THEY CURSE HIM DAILY**

Rating 1 2 3 4 5 Date Used: _____

283. IT IS BETTER TO
SPEAK TRUTH THAN
BE PURSUED BY
REGRETS

Rating 1 2 3 4 5 Date Used: _____

284. DON'T SETTLE FOR
THE STATUS QUO
AFTER THE QUO
HAS LOST ITS STATUS

Rating 1 2 3 4 5 Date Used: _____

285. CHANGING ONES MIND
IS NOT A SIN
IT SIMPLY SAYS WE
ARE NOW WISER

Rating 1 2 3 4 5 Date Used: _____

286. LOVE CURES PEOPLE
BOTH THE GIVER
AND THE RECEIVER

Rating 1 2 3 4 5 Date Used: _____

287. PEOPLE WHO THROW
MUD AT OTHERS
ALWAYS GET DIRTIER

Rating 1 2 3 4 5 Date Used: _____

288. TRUTH CAN UNDERSTAND ERROR BUT ERROR CAN'T UNDERSTAND TRUTH
— G.K. CHESTERTON

Rating 1 2 3 4 5 Date Used: _____

289. HUMAN RIGHTS HAVE SPIRITUAL ROOTS NOT RACIAL ONES

Rating 1 2 3 4 5 Date Used: _____

290. THE PEACE OF GOD IS MORE VALUABLE THAN ALL THE RICHES BEYOND THE GRASP OF THE POOR

Rating 1 2 3 4 5 Date Used: _____

291. POLITICIANS RARELY FORGIVE PUTTING PRINCIPLE AHEAD OF THEIR PARTY

Rating 1 2 3 4 5 Date Used: _____

292. GOD DOESN'T TWEET, BLOG, OR DO FACEBOOK BUT HE DOES HEAR YOUR PRAYERS

Rating 1 2 3 4 5 Date Used: _____

293. ALL GREAT LIES HAVE AN ELEMENT OF PERVERTED TRUTH AT THE CORE

Rating 1 2 3 4 5 Date Used: _____

294. GOD SENDS NO STRESS THAT PRAYER AND A LITTLE CHOCOLATE CAN'T OVERCOME

Rating 1 2 3 4 5 Date Used: _____

295. WHEN TROUBLE COMES CHARACTER SHOWS

Rating 1 2 3 4 5 Date Used: _____

296. WE CAN'T HOLD OTHERS ACCOUNTABLE FOR STANDARDS WE REFUSE TO MEET

Rating 1 2 3 4 5 Date Used: _____

297. SATAN: MY GREATEST ACCOMPLISHMENT IS TO CONVINCE PEOPLE I DON'T EXIST

Rating 1 2 3 4 5 Date Used: _____

298. TRUST IS THE RESIDUE OF PROMISES KEPT

Rating 1 2 3 4 5 Date Used: _____

299. ONLY GREAT MEN HAVE GREAT FAULTS
— FRENCH PROVERB

Rating 1 2 3 4 5 Date Used: _____

300. REASON MAKES MISTAKES CONSCIENCE NEVER DOES

Rating 1 2 3 4 5 Date Used: _____

301. THE TROUBLE WITH AN OPEN MIND IS THAT PEOPLE ALWAYS WANT TO FILL IT

Rating 1 2 3 4 5 Date Used: _____

302. A GOOD LAWYER KNOWS THE LAW; A CLEVER ONE TAKES THE JUDGE TO LUNCH

Rating 1 2 3 4 5 Date Used: _____

303. THE PAST SHOULD NEVER HOLD THE FUTURE HOSTAGE

Rating   1   2   3   4   5   Date Used: _____

304. THERE ARE NONE SO BLIND AS THOSE WHO CANNOT SEE SIN

Rating   1   2   3   4   5   Date Used: _____

305. ISLAM IS A RELIGION OF PEACE AND LOVE AND SOME WILL KILL YOU TO PROVE IT

Rating   1   2   3   4   5   Date Used: _____

306. FAILURE IS NOT A CRIME – FAILING TO TRY IS

Rating   1   2   3   4   5   Date Used: _____

307. FALLING APART IS NOT A SIN FAILING TO REBUILD IS

Rating   1   2   3   4   5   Date Used: _____

308. THOSE WHO DO NOT
ASK DO NOT LEARN

Rating 1 2 3 4 5 Date Used: _____

309. WHEN TROUBLE GROWS
CHARACTER SHOWS

Rating 1 2 3 4 5 Date Used: _____

310. TROUBLE THAT DRIVES
YOU CLOSER TO JESUS IS
A PRICELESS TREASURE

Rating 1 2 3 4 5 Date Used: _____

311. THE WHOLE UNIVERSE
IS BUT THE FOOTPRINT
OF DIVINE GOODNESS
— DANTE

Rating 1 2 3 4 5 Date Used: _____

312. YOU MUST SCALE THE
MOUNTAIN IF YOU
VIEW THE PLAIN
— CHINESE PROVERB

Rating 1 2 3 4 5 Date Used: _____

313. LAUGHTER CURES
MANY ILLS AND HEALS
RELATIONSHIPS

Rating 1 2 3 4 5 Date Used: _____

314. TO ENVY ANOTHER IS TO DIMINISH ONESELF

Rating 1 2 3 4 5 Date Used: _____

315. A SELF-MADE MAN WORSHIPS HIS CREATOR

Rating 1 2 3 4 5 Date Used: _____

316. THE BAD NEWS IS TIME FLIES THE GOOD NEWS IS YOU ARE THE PILOT

Rating 1 2 3 4 5 Date Used: _____

317. TO REALLY FEEL WEALTHY COUNT THE BLESSINGS MONEY CAN'T BUY

Rating 1 2 3 4 5 Date Used: _____

318. MOTHER IS A VERB NOT A NOUN

Rating 1 2 3 4 5 Date Used: _____

319. NEVER CONFUSE A SINGLE DEFEAT WITH A LOST WAR

Rating 1 2 3 4 5 Date Used: _____

320. MONEY BUYS EVERYTHING EXCEPT, SALVATION, LOVE, PEACE, INTEGRITY, AND TRUE FRIENDSHIP

Rating 1 2 3 4 5   Date Used: _____

321. THE MORE THE TREE IS PRUNED THE BETTER THE FRUIT

Rating 1 2 3 4 5   Date Used: _____

322. FEAR AND LOVE DO NOT WALK TOGETHER

Rating 1 2 3 4 5   Date Used: _____

323. THE UPPER CRUST IS A BUNCH OF CRUMBS HELD TOGETHER BY DOUGH — J.A. THOMAS

Rating 1 2 3 4 5   Date Used: _____

324. PRAYER WILL END SIN OR SIN WILL END PRAYER IT'S OUR CHOICE

Rating 1 2 3 4 5   Date Used: _____

325. IF CHRIST IS RISEN NOTHING ELSE MATTERS IF CHRIST IS NOT RISEN NOTHING MATTERS

Rating 1 2 3 4 5 Date Used: _____

326. WHAT WE GET MAKES A LIVING, WHAT WE GIVE MAKES A LIFE — W. CHURCHILL

Rating 1 2 3 4 5 Date Used: _____

327. A CLEAR CONSCIENCE IS THE SIGN OF A BAD MEMORY — MARK TWAIN

Rating 1 2 3 4 5 Date Used: _____

328. CREATIVITY AND SUCCESS CAN BE KILLED BY THE FEAR OF FAILURE

Rating 1 2 3 4 5 Date Used: _____

329. NOBLE FATHERS HAVE NOBLE CHILDREN — EURIPIDES

Rating 1 2 3 4 5 Date Used: _____

330. **A HAPPY FAMILY IS BUT AN EARLIER HEAVEN — JOHN BROWNING**

Rating 1 2 3 4 5 Date Used: _____

331. **NO CHRISTIAN STANDS TALLER THAN WHEN THEY KNEEL**

Rating 1 2 3 4 5 Date Used: _____

332. **GOOD FRIENDS ARE ONE OF GOD'S GREATEST BLESSINGS**

Rating 1 2 3 4 5 Date Used: _____

333. **IT'S BETTER TO FOLD OUR HANDS THAN TO WRING THEM**

Rating 1 2 3 4 5 Date Used: _____

334. **GOD BLESSES EVEN IN OUR MESSES**

Rating 1 2 3 4 5 Date Used: _____

335. DON'T TELL GOD HOW BIG THE STORM IS UNTIL YOU TELL THE STORM HOW BIG YOUR GOD IS

Rating   1   2   3   4   5   Date Used: _____

336. IF JESUS IS A STRANGER CHECK YOUR CIRCLE OF FRIENDS

Rating   1   2   3   4   5   Date Used: _____

337. UNLESS WE HAVE IN US THAT WHICH IS ABOVE US WE WILL YIELD TO THAT BENEATH US

Rating   1   2   3   4   5   Date Used: _____

338. IT TAKES A PEACE WITHIN BEFORE A PERSON CAN LIVE IN PEACE WITH OTHERS

Rating   1   2   3   4   5   Date Used: _____

339. IT TAKES AN OPEN MIND TO HAVE AN OPEN HEART

Rating   1   2   3   4   5   Date Used: _____

340. STOP CHASING THE WRONG THINGS AND GOOD THINGS WILL CATCH UP TO YOU

Rating   1   2   3   4   5   Date Used: _____

341. SOME OF GOD'S GREATEST GIFTS ARE UNANSWERED PRAYERS — GARTH BROOKS

Rating   1   2   3   4   5   Date Used: _____

342. LOST HOPE IS AN UNDERTAKERS BEST FRIEND

Rating   1   2   3   4   5   Date Used: _____

343. THE REAL TRICK IN LIFE IS TO STAY ALIVE AS LONG AS YOU LIVE

Rating   1   2   3   4   5   Date Used: _____

344. THOSE WHO LOVE DEEPLY NEVER GROW OLD THEY STAY YOUNG EVEN IN OLD AGE

Rating   1   2   3   4   5   Date Used: _____

345. FOR THE UNWISE
OLD AGE IS WINTER
FOR THE WISE IT IS
HARVEST TIME

Rating 1 2 3 4 5 Date Used: _____

346. IT'S HARD TO STUMBLE
WHEN YOU ARE
WALKING HAND
IN HAND

Rating 1 2 3 4 5 Date Used: _____

347. THE PLEASURE OF DOING
GOOD IS THE ONLY ONE
THAT WILL NOT WEAR OUT
— CHINESE PROVERB

Rating 1 2 3 4 5 Date Used: _____

348. WORRY IS LIKE A
ROCKING CHAIR IT
MOVES YOU BUT
GOES NOWHERE

Rating 1 2 3 4 5 Date Used: _____

349. LIVE AS IF EVERYTING
WAS RIGGED IN YOUR
FAVOR BECAUSE, IF
YOU LOVE JESUS, IT IS

Rating 1 2 3 4 5 Date Used: _____

350. YOUR HOME SHOULD
BE THE ANTEDOTE TO
STRESS NOT ITS CAUSE
— PETER WALSH

Rating   1   2   3   4   5   Date Used: _____

351. GRACE MEETS US
WHERE WE ARE AND
TAKES US TO A
GLORIOUS FUTURE

Rating   1   2   3   4   5   Date Used: _____

352. ACCOMMODATE CHANGING
TIMES BUT NEVER
CHANGING VALUES

Rating   1   2   3   4   5   Date Used: _____

353. THERE IS NO LUCK
EXCEPT WHERE THERE
IS DISCIPLINE
— IRISH PROVERB

Rating   1   2   3   4   5   Date Used: _____

354. LOVE IS CONTAGIOUS
INFECT AS MANY AS
YOU POSSIBLY CAN

Rating   1   2   3   4   5   Date Used: _____

355. IN AN AGE OF CHANGE
NOTHING IS MORE
IMPORTANT THAN
UNCHANGING TRUTH

Rating 1 2 3 4 5 Date Used: _____

356. WE CAN'T BE WHAT GOD
WANTS US TO BE IF
WE STAY AS WE ARE

Rating 1 2 3 4 5 Date Used: _____

357. YOU CAN'T STAND STILL
IN THE CHRISTIAN
FAITH; ITS EITHER
FORWARD OR BACKWARD

Rating 1 2 3 4 5 Date Used: _____

358. HOPE SEES THE INVISIBLE,
FEELS THE INTANGIBLE,
AND ACHEIVES
THE IMPOSSIBLE

Rating 1 2 3 4 5 Date Used: _____

359. HE THAT SEES THE
INVISIBLE CAN DO
THE IMPOSSIBLE
— JOHN HAGGAI

Rating 1 2 3 4 5 Date Used: _____

360. GIVE LOVE IT'S THE ONLY THING YOU'LL NEVER RUN OUT OF

Rating 1 2 3 4 5 Date Used: _____

361. DON'T BE A PORCH SWING PERSON IN A HURRY UP WORLD

Rating 1 2 3 4 5 Date Used: _____

362. IF YOU CAN DREAM ABOUT IT DON'T DO IT

Rating 1 2 3 4 5 Date Used: _____

363. LEARNING IS GOOD APPLYING IT IS BETTER

Rating 1 2 3 4 5 Date Used: _____

364. BELIEVE SOMETHING UNSEEN IS CARING FOR YOU – IT'S A LIFE ENRICHING THOUGHT

Rating 1 2 3 4 5 Date Used: _____

365. IF YOU WANT TO GO FAST, GO ALONE. IF YOU WANT TO GO FAR GO TOGETHER

Rating 1 2 3 4 5 Date Used: _____

366. IF THE WIND WILL NOT SERVE TAKE THE OARS — LATIN PROVERB

Rating 1 2 3 4 5 Date Used: _____

367. DO NOT FROWN IF SMILES ARE AVAILABLE

Rating 1 2 3 4 5 Date Used: _____

368. PEOPLE WHO DON'T WANT THE BEST FOR YOU AREN'T THE BEST FOR YOU

Rating 1 2 3 4 5 Date Used: _____

369. DON'T BE DISCOURAGED. ITS OFTEN THE LAST KEY IN THE BUNCH THAT OPENS THE LOCK

Rating 1 2 3 4 5 Date Used: _____

370. PROGRESS IS OFTEN MADE BY LAZY MEN TRYING TO FIND AN EASIER WAY

Rating 1 2 3 4 5 Date Used: _____

371. A LEADER WITHOUT FOLLOWERS IS JUST A PERSON OUT FOR A WALK

Rating 1 2 3 4 5 Date Used: _____

372. IT IS BETTER TO DIE FOR SOMETHING THAN TO LIVE FOR NOTHING

Rating 1 2 3 4 5 Date Used: _____

373. THE SIMPLE ACT OF CARING IS HEROIC
— EDWARD ALBERT

Rating 1 2 3 4 5 Date Used: _____

374. HEARING SOMEONE RATHER THAN JUST LISTENING IS AN ACT OF LOVE

Rating 1 2 3 4 5 Date Used: _____

375. ETHICAL BEHAVIOR DOESN'T TAKE THE FUN OUT OF LIFE IT INCREASES IT

Rating 1 2 3 4 5 Date Used: _____

376. ONE MINUTE OF PATIENCE, TEN YEARS OF PEACE
— GREEK PROVERB

Rating   1   2   3   4   5   Date Used: _____

377. ONE IDEA IN ACTION IS WORTH TEN IN REFLECTION

Rating   1   2   3   4   5   Date Used: _____

378. PREPARE AND PREVENT DON'T REPAIR AND REPENT

Rating   1   2   3   4   5   Date Used: _____

379. GOD'S ANSWERS ARE WISER THAN OUR PRAYERS

Rating   1   2   3   4   5   Date Used: _____

380. DON'T PRAY JUST WHEN YOU FEEL LIKE IT
WE HAVE POWER ON OUR KNEES

Rating   1   2   3   4   5   Date Used: _____

381. PRAYER IS A WEAPON
OF THE CHRISTIAN
CHURCH USE IT OFTEN
AND EFFECTIVELY

Rating 1 2 3 4 5 Date Used: _____

382. WHETHER YOU BELIEVE
YOU CAN OR CAN'T
YOU ARE RIGHT
— HENRY FORD

Rating 1 2 3 4 5 Date Used: _____

383. DON'T RESIGN YOURSELF
TO YOUR FATE – YOUR
RESIGNATION MAY BE
ACCEPTED

Rating 1 2 3 4 5 Date Used: _____

384. STRESS CANNOT EXIST
IN THE PRESENCE
OF CHOCOLATE

Rating 1 2 3 4 5 Date Used: _____

385. DOING NOTHING IS
VERY HARD BECAUSE
YOU NEVER FINISH
AND ACCOMPLISH ZERO

Rating 1 2 3 4 5 Date Used: _____

386. YOUR VALUE HAS NOTHING TO DO WITH YOUR VALUABLES
— RICK WARREN

Rating 1 2 3 4 5 Date Used: _____

387. SINCE LIFE IS A BUMPY ROAD CONSIDER USING LAUGHTER AS SHOCK ABSORBER

Rating 1 2 3 4 5 Date Used: _____

388. THERE IS NEVER A WRONG TIME TO DO THE RIGHT THING

Rating 1 2 3 4 5 Date Used: _____

389. GOD IS OUR POTTER TIRELESSLY SEEKING TO PERFECT US

Rating 1 2 3 4 5 Date Used: _____

390. FAILING TO FORGIVE ALLOWS SIN TO OCCUPY SPACE IN YOUR MIND RENT-FREE

Rating 1 2 3 4 5 Date Used: _____

391. GOOD CHARACTER IS PRICELESS, NEVER SELL IT OR GIVE IT AWAY

Rating 1 2 3 4 5 Date Used: _____

392. A MOTHER'S LOVE IS JUST A SMALL SAMPLE OF WHAT GOD HAS FOR US

Rating 1 2 3 4 5 Date Used: _____

393. GOOD JOKES ARE LIKE OLD FRIENDS THEY SHOULD BE REVISITED NOW AND THEN

Rating 1 2 3 4 5 Date Used: _____

394. MORE LIKE THE MASTER WE SHOULD WANT TO BE

Rating 1 2 3 4 5 Date Used: _____

395. OUR VALUE IS DETERMINED MORE BY WHAT WE GIVE THAN BY WHAT WE GET

Rating 1 2 3 4 5 Date Used: _____

396.   WHEN COMPASSION
DEPARTS SO DOES
HUMANITY

Rating 1 2 3 4 5 Date Used: _____

397.   EVEN A SMALL
THORN CAUSES
FESTERING
— IRISH PROVERB

Rating 1 2 3 4 5 Date Used: _____

398.   DON'T SMOTHER OTHERS
NO ONE CAN GROW
IN THE SHADE
— LEO BUSCAGLIA

Rating 1 2 3 4 5 Date Used: _____

399.   WHERE THERE IS NO
LAW THERE IS NO
LIBERTY
— JOHN LOCKE

Rating 1 2 3 4 5 Date Used: _____

400.   RECOCILIATION WITH
THE FATHER MEANS WE
WILL NEVER BE ALONE

Rating 1 2 3 4 5 Date Used: _____

401. NOBODY WORKS AS HARD AS A LAZY PERSON

Rating 1 2 3 4 5 Date Used: _____

402. WHAT EVER FOLLOWS "I AM" IS GOING TO COME LOOKING FOR YOU — JOEL OSTEEN

Rating 1 2 3 4 5 Date Used: _____

403. TWO WONDERFUL GIFTS FROM GOD: TRUE FRIENDS AND TRUE LOVE

Rating 1 2 3 4 5 Date Used: _____

404. SOME PEOPLE WITH MONEY AREN'T RICH SOME PEOPLE WITHOUT MONEY ARE RICH

Rating 1 2 3 4 5 Date Used: _____

405. GOD DOESN'T LOVE US BECAUSE WE ARE GOOD, HIS LOVE MAKES US GOOD

Rating 1 2 3 4 5 Date Used: _____

406. GOD LOVES CHEERFUL GIVERS NOT CHEERFUL GETTERS

Rating   1   2   3   4   5   Date Used: _____

407. HEAVENLY REWARDS WILL BE BASED ON WHAT WE GAVE NOT WHAT WE GOT

Rating   1   2   3   4   5   Date Used: _____

408. THE FAMILY IS ONE OF GOD'S MASTERPIECES

Rating   1   2   3   4   5   Date Used: _____

409. WORK SPARES US FROM THREE EVILS: BOREDON, VICE, AND NEED

Rating   1   2   3   4   5   Date Used: _____

410. LOVE CANNOT LIVE WHERE THERE IS NOT TRUST
— EDITH HAMILTON

Rating   1   2   3   4   5   Date Used: _____

411. NO ONE KNOWS LESS THAN THE PERSON WHO KNOWS IT ALL
— HUGH GLOSTER

Rating 1 2 3 4 5 Date Used: _____

412. A PERSON WITHOUT HUMOR IS LIKE A WAGON WITHOUT SPRINGS

Rating 1 2 3 4 5 Date Used: _____

413. DO NOT FEAR FAILURE SOMETHING GOOD OFTEN COMES FROM IT

Rating 1 2 3 4 5 Date Used: _____

414. FORGET POKEMON "GO" FIND JESUS

Rating 1 2 3 4 5 Date Used: _____

415. HOPE IS A VERB WITH ITS SHIRTSLEEVES ROLLED UP
— DAVID ORR

Rating 1 2 3 4 5 Date Used: _____

416. **TRUE INNER PEACE CAN ONLY COME FROM OUR CREATOR**

Rating 1 2 3 4 5 Date Used: _____

417. **PEARLS DON'T LIE ON THE SEASHORE YOU MUST DIVE FOR THEM — CHINESE PROVERB**

Rating 1 2 3 4 5 Date Used: _____

418. **SPIRITUALLY MINDED PEOPLE STAY GROUNDED AMID THE CLUTTER OF SECULAR TRIBULATION**

Rating 1 2 3 4 5 Date Used: _____

419. **OPEN MINDED PEOPLE RISK HAVING THEIR BRAINS FALL OUT**

Rating 1 2 3 4 5 Date Used: _____

420. **WORDS GET ATTENTION BUT ACTIONS PERSUADE**

Rating 1 2 3 4 5 Date Used: _____

421. **DO ONE THING EVERY DAY THAT SCARES YOU — ELEANOR ROOSEVELT**

Rating 1 2 3 4 5 Date Used: _____

422. LIFELONG LEARNING LEADS TO LIFE LONG GROWTH

Rating 1 2 3 4 5 Date Used: _____

423. WISE PEOPLE SEPARATE ESSENTIALS FROM NON ESSENTIALS AND DON'T SWEAT THE LATTER

Rating 1 2 3 4 5 Date Used: _____

424. COMMON SENSE AND JOY ARE RELATED COMMON SENSE PROMOTES JOY

Rating 1 2 3 4 5 Date Used: _____

425. LIVE TODAY SO YOUR MEMORIES WILL BRING HAPPINESS TOMORROW

Rating 1 2 3 4 5 Date Used: _____

426. BUILD A FUTURE – DON'T JUST POLISH THE PAST

Rating 1 2 3 4 5 Date Used: _____

427. GO WHERE YOUR
      BEST PRAYERS TAKE
      YOU
      — FREDERICK BUECHNER

Rating 1 2 3 4 5 Date Used: _____

428. THE WISE WALK
      SOFTLY AND CARRY
      BIG TRUTHS

Rating 1 2 3 4 5 Date Used: _____

429. WHEN YOU STAND
      ALONE FOR TRUTH
      SMILE BECAUSE
      GOD DOES

Rating 1 2 3 4 5 Date Used: _____

430. IF YOU CAN'T
      CONVINCE THEM
      CONFUSE THEM
      — AUTHOR UNKNOWN

Rating 1 2 3 4 5 Date Used: _____

431. GRIEF DOES NOT
      CHANGE YOU IT
      REVEALS YOU
      — JOHN GREEN

Rating 1 2 3 4 5 Date Used: _____

432. THOSE WHO DONOT
BELIEVE IN GOD WILL
BELIEVE IN ANYTHING

Rating 1 2 3 4 5 Date Used: _____

433. THE BILL FOR HINDSIGHT
IS HIGHER THAN THE
PROFIT FROM FORESIGHT

Rating 1 2 3 4 5 Date Used: _____

434. BID FARWELL TO
DISCIPLINE AND YOU
SAY GOODBY TO SUCCESS
—ALEX FURGESON

Rating 1 2 3 4 5 Date Used: _____

435. LET YOUR HOPES
NOT YOOUR HURTS
SHAPE YOUR FUTURE

Rating 1 2 3 4 5 Date Used: _____

436. CREATE A BIG CEMETERY
IN WHICH TO BURY THE
FAULTS OF YOUR
FRIENDS

Rating 1 2 3 4 5 Date Used: _____

437. YOU HAVE AS MUCH
LAUGHTER AS YOU
HAVE FAITH
— MARTIN LUTHER

Rating 1 2 3 4 5 Date Used: _____

438. BEWARE OF THE HALF
TRUTH YOU MAY
HAVE THE WRONG HALF

Rating 1 2 3 4 5 Date Used: _____

439. TO SEE EVIL AND
NOT CALL IT EVIL
IS EVIL
— D. BONOFFER

Rating 1 2 3 4 5 Date Used: _____

440. THANKSGIVING MEANS
NOTHING UNLESS IT
LEADS TO THANKSLIVING

Rating 1 2 3 4 5 Date Used: _____

441. IN LIFE IT'S NOT THE
SPEED THAT COUNTS
IT'S THE DIRECTION

Rating 1 2 3 4 5 Date Used: _____

442. AN INVESTMENT IN
KNOWLEDGE PAYS
THE BEST INTEREST
— BEN FRANKLIN

Rating   1   2   3   4   5   Date Used: _____

443. VIRTUE IN NOT LEFT
TO STAND ALONE GOD
WILL SEND FRIENDS

Rating   1   2   3   4   5   Date Used: _____

444. TRY TO BE A RAINBOW
TO SOMEONE'S CLOUD
— MAYA ANGELO

Rating   1   2   3   4   5   Date Used: _____

445. CRIES FOR HELP ARE
FREQUENTLY INAUDIBLE
— TOM ROBBINS

Rating   1   2   3   4   5   Date Used: _____

446. STAND UP FOR WHAT
IS RIGHT BECAUSE
GOD WILL STAND
WITH YOU

Rating   1   2   3   4   5   Date Used: _____

447. WHEN WE SAY "I"
"ME" AND "MY"
TOO MUCH "WE"
AND "OUR" GET LOST

Rating 1 2 3 4 5 Date Used: _____

448. MAKING OURSELVES
HAPPY OR SAD TAKES
THE SAME AMOUNT
OF WORK

Rating 1 2 3 4 5 Date Used: _____

449. WHETHER YOUR CUP
IS HALF EMPTY OR
HALF FULL BE
THANKFUL FOR THE CUP

Rating 1 2 3 4 5 Date Used: _____

450. WHEN FEAR KNOCKS ON
YOUR DOOR SEND FAITH
TO ANSWER AND FEAR
WILL LEAVE

Rating 1 2 3 4 5 Date Used: _____

451. JOY IS THE HOLY FIRE
THAT KEEPS OUR PURPOSE
WARM AND INTELLIGENCE
A GLOW — HELEN KELLER

Rating 1 2 3 4 5 Date Used: _____

452. WASTE NOT FRESH TEARS OVER OLD GRIEFS
— EURIPIDES

Rating 1 2 3 4 5 Date Used: _____

453. ALL THE ROADS LEADING TO SUCCESS PASS THROUGH HARD WORK JUNCTION

Rating 1 2 3 4 5 Date Used: _____

454. OUR ACTIONS DISPLAY THE DEPTH OF OUR FAITH

Rating 1 2 3 4 5 Date Used: _____

455. THE BEST GIFTS AT CHRISTMAS ARE GIVEN WITH AUTHENIC LOVE

Rating 1 2 3 4 5 Date Used: _____

456. A MERRY CHRISTMAS IS A BRIDGE TO A HAPPY NEW YEAR

Rating 1 2 3 4 5 Date Used: _____

457. RING HAPPY BELLS
ACROSS THE SNOW THIS
YEAR IS GOING LET IT GO
— LORD TENNYSON

Rating   1   2   3   4   5   Date Used: _____

458. HABIT RULES THE
UNREFLECTING HERD
—WILLIAM WORDSWORTH

Rating   1   2   3   4   5   Date Used: _____

459. IF YOU SEE SOMETHING
STUPID CHANGE IT
— NEWT GINGRICH

Rating   1   2   3   4   5   Date Used: _____

460. COURAGE IS FEAR THAT
HANGS ON A LITTLE LONGER

Rating   1   2   3   4   5   Date Used: _____

461. TOO MUCH OF A
GOOD THING ISN'T
A GOOD THING
— KATHY KOCH

Rating   1   2   3   4   5   Date Used: _____

462. EVERY CHILD WAS
CREATED ON PURPOSE
WITH PURPOSE
— KATHY KOCH

Rating 1 2 3 4 5 Date Used: _____

463. SHOW ME YOUR FRIENDS
AND I WILL SHOW
YOU YOUR FUTURE
— KATHY KOCH

Rating 1 2 3 4 5 Date Used: _____

464. STRENGHTS NOT
HARNESSED CAN
BECOME WEAKNESSES
— KATHY KOCH

Rating 1 2 3 4 5 Date Used: _____

465. IF YOU TELL A BIG
LIE OFTEN ENOUGH
IT WILL BECOME TRUTH
— JOSEPH GOEBBELS

Rating 1 2 3 4 5 Date Used: _____

466. LOOK NOT BACK IN
ANGER OR AHEAD IN
FEAR RATHER LOOK
AROUND IN HOPE

Rating 1 2 3 4 5 Date Used: _____

467. DON'T FOCUS ON ANSWERS UNTIL YOU'RE CERTAIN THE QUESTION IS APPROPRIATE

Rating 1 2 3 4 5 Date Used: _____

468. LEARN FROM YOUR PAST DON'T RELIVE IT

Rating 1 2 3 4 5 Date Used: _____

469. THERE IS NO PRIZE WITHOUT A COST
— JOHN HAGEE

Rating 1 2 3 4 5 Date Used: _____

470. YOU WILL EITHER STEP FORWARD INTO GROWTH OR BACKWARD IINTO SAFETY

Rating 1 2 3 4 5 Date Used: _____

471. ONE'S TRUE METTLE IS THE TIMES YOU TRY BEFORE QUITTING

Rating 1 2 3 4 5 Date Used: _____

472. THE BEGINNING OF HEALTH IS TO KNOW THE DISEASE
— SPANISH PROVERB

Rating 1 2 3 4 5 Date Used: _____

473. THE ONE THING PEOPLE SHOULD NEVER BE WILLING TO SELL IS CHARACTER

Rating 1 2 3 4 5 Date Used: _____

474. KEEP WORKING, KEEP STRIVING, NEVER GIVE UP FALL 7 TIMES, GET UP 8
— DENZEL WASHINGTON

Rating 1 2 3 4 5 Date Used: _____

475. ONE PERSON STANDING ON THE WORD OF GOD IS THE MAJORITY
— MAYA ANGELO

Rating 1 2 3 4 5 Date Used: _____

476. SERVICE IS GOD'S LOVE IN WORK CLOTHES
— JOHN HAGEE

Rating 1 2 3 4 5 Date Used: _____

477. IT WAS THEIR FAITH IN GOD THAT BUILT THIS COUNTRY
— RONALD REAGAN

Rating 1 2 3 4 5 Date Used: _____

478. WITHOUT MORALS A REPUBLIC CANNOT SUBSIST ANY LENGTH OF TIME
— CHARLES CARROLL

Rating 1 2 3 4 5   Date Used: _____

479. I SEE JESUS IN EVERY HUMAN BEING
— MOTHER TERESA

Rating 1 2 3 4 5   Date Used: _____

480. I SERVE BECAUSE I LOVE JESUS
— MOTHER TERESA

Rating 1 2 3 4 5   Date Used: _____

481. IN THE U.S. CHRISTIANITY IS MOSTLY EVERY WHERE THE SAME
— ALEXIS de TOCQUEVILLE

Rating 1 2 3 4 5   Date Used: _____

482. THE LONGER I LIVE ... I SEE PROOF THAT GOD GOVERNS ....
— BEN FRANKLIN

Rating 1 2 3 4 5   Date Used: _____

483. THE 1ST AMENDMENT WAS WRITTEN TO PROTECT RELIGION FROM GOV'T.
— RONALD REAGAN

Rating 1 2 3 4 5 Date Used: _____

484. NOTHING IN THE 1ST AMEND. CONVERTS SCHOOLS INTO RELIGIOUS FREE ZONES
— BILL CLINTON

Rating 1 2 3 4 5 Date Used: _____

485. THE GOD WHO GAVE US LIFE GAVE US LIBERTY
— THOMAS JEFFERSON

Rating 1 2 3 4 5 Date Used: _____

486. AMERICANS TOLERATE EVERY RELIGIOUS GROUP EXCEPT THEIR OWN

Rating 1 2 3 4 5 Date Used: _____

487. GOD'S DELAYS ARE NOT GOD'S DENIALS
— JOHN HAGEE

Rating 1 2 3 4 5 Date Used: _____

488. **SETBACKS BECOME COMEBACKS WHEN GOD IS IN IT**

Rating 1 2 3 4 5 Date Used: _____

489. **A NEAR NEIGHBOR IS BETTER THAN A DISTANT COUSIN — ITALIAN PROVERB**

Rating 1 2 3 4 5 Date Used: _____

490. **WHAT RIPENS FAST DOESN'T LAST — GERMAN PROVERB**

Rating 1 2 3 4 5 Date Used: _____

491. **AGING IS NOT LOST YOUTH BUT A NEW STAGE OF GROWTH AND OPPORTUNITY**

Rating 1 2 3 4 5 Date Used: _____

492. **DON'T LET YOUR YESTERDAYS HOLD YOUR TOMORROWS HOSTAGE**

Rating 1 2 3 4 5 Date Used: _____

493. FAILURE CANNOT DEFINE YOU IF YOU LEARN FROM IT

Rating 1 2 3 4 5 Date Used: _____

494. ALWAYS BORROW MONEY FROM A PESSIMIST HE WON'T EXPECT IT BACK
— OSCAR WILDE

Rating 1 2 3 4 5 Date Used: _____

495. ONLY HE WHO CAN SEE THE INVISIBLE CAN DO THE IMPOSSIBLE
— FRANK GAINES

Rating 1 2 3 4 5 Date Used: _____

496. WE REVEAL OUR CHARACTER BY WHAT WE SHARE WITH OTHERS

Rating 1 2 3 4 5 Date Used: _____

497. BETWEEN SAYING AND DOING MANY A PAIR OF SHOES IS WORN OUT
— ITALIAN PROVERB

Rating 1 2 3 4 5 Date Used: _____

498. WORDS EMPTY AS THE WIND ARE BEST LEFT UNSAID
— HOMER

Rating 1 2 3 4 5   Date Used: _____

499. IF YOU HAVE 6 HOURS TO CHOP DOWN A TREE SPEND 4 HOURS SHARPENING THE AXE

Rating 1 2 3 4 5   Date Used: _____

500. MONEY IS A GREAT SERVANT BUT A HORRIBLE MASTER

Rating 1 2 3 4 5   Date Used: _____

501. BE THE SILENCE THAT LISTENS
— TARA BRACH

Rating 1 2 3 4 5   Date Used: _____

502. A PROBLEM IS A TERRIBLE THING TO WASTE

Rating 1 2 3 4 5   Date Used: _____

503. THE PURPOSE OF LIFE
IS A LIFE OF PURPOSE
— ROBERT BYRNE

Rating 1 2 3 4 5 Date Used: _____

504. SOCIALISM'S INHERENT
VIRTUE IS THE EQUAL
SHAREING OF MISERY
— WINSTON CHURCHILL

Rating 1 2 3 4 5 Date Used: _____

505. MANY A FALSE STEP
HAS BEEN MADE BY
STANDING STILL

Rating 1 2 3 4 5 Date Used: _____

506. HAPPINESS IS WANTING
WHAT YOU HAVE

Rating 1 2 3 4 5 Date Used: _____

507. THE WORLD IS CHANGED
BY EXAMPLES NOT
BY OPINIONS

Rating 1 2 3 4 5 Date Used: _____

508. CYNICISM IS A DISEASE
THAT ROBS PEOPLE
OF THE GIFT OF LIFE

Rating 1 2 3 4 5 Date Used: _____

509. THEY TRIED TO BURY US BUT DIDN'T KNOW WE WERE SEEDS — MEXICAN PROVERB

Rating 1 2 3 4 5 Date Used: _____

510. WE CAN'T BE BUTTERFLYS UNTIL WE QUIT BEING CATERPILLARS

Rating 1 2 3 4 5 Date Used: _____

511. EASTER IS LOVE EASTER BRINGS PEACE, HOPE, JOY AND AN ETERNITY WITH GOD

Rating 1 2 3 4 5 Date Used: _____

512. ENOUGH IS AS GOOD AS A FEAST

Rating 1 2 3 4 5 Date Used: _____

513. A MATURE CHRISTIAN IS ONE WHOSE LOVE FOR OTHERS OUTWEIGHS SELF CONCERN

Rating 1 2 3 4 5 Date Used: _____

514. THE TRUTH SPOKEN TOO LATE IS WORSE THAN A LIE

Rating 1 2 3 4 5 Date Used: _____

515. HOPE IS PATIENCE WITH THE LAMP LIT
— TERTULIAN

Rating 1 2 3 4 5 Date Used: _____

516. WHILE WAITING FOR THE STORM TO PASS LEARN TO DANCE IN THE RAIN

Rating 1 2 3 4 5 Date Used: _____

517. SOLITUDE IS THE SOUL'S HOLIDAY AND A CHANCE FOR SELF RENEWAL

Rating 1 2 3 4 5 Date Used: _____

518. BE A LIGHTHOUSE CREATED TO SERVE SERVING BY SHINING ALTRUISM IN ACTION

Rating 1 2 3 4 5 Date Used: _____

519. BE A LIGHTHOUSE
PROJECT CHRIST'S
LIGHT AND LOVE

Rating 1 2 3 4 5 Date Used: _____

520. KINDNESS IS IN OUR
POWER EVEN WHEN
FONDNESS IS NOT
— SAMUEL JOHNSON

Rating 1 2 3 4 5 Date Used: _____

521. YOUR ASSUMPTIONS
MUST BE RIGHT
FOR YOU TO BE

Rating 1 2 3 4 5 Date Used: _____

522. BROODING IS THE
MOTHER OF
INEFFECTIVENESS
— MAJ SJOWALL

Rating 1 2 3 4 5 Date Used: _____

523. FEELINGS AND EMOTIONS
CAN MISLEAD
REASON AND TRUTH
CANNOT

Rating 1 2 3 4 5 Date Used: _____

524. LIFE DOESN'T IMITATE ART IT IMITATES BAD TELEVISION
— WOODY ALLEN

Rating 1 2 3 4 5 Date Used: _____

525. A PEACOCK THAT RESTS ON HIS FEATHERS IS JUST ANOTHER TURKEY
— DOLLY PARTON

Rating 1 2 3 4 5 Date Used: _____

526. THE CHRISTIAN SHOULD COMFORT THE AFFLICTED AND AFFLICT THE COMFORTABLE

Rating 1 2 3 4 5 Date Used: _____

527. EVERY DAY SHOULD BE OUR HEAVENLY FATHER'S DAY THANK GOD

Rating 1 2 3 4 5 Date Used: _____

528. ONLY IN A STORM CAN WE KNOW GOD'S GREATNESS
— JOHN HAGEE

Rating 1 2 3 4 5 Date Used: _____

529.   **A PROMISE IS ONLY AS GOOD AS THE PERSON WHO MAKES IT**

Rating   1   2   3   4   5   Date Used: _____

530.   **THE STRUGGLE OF TODAY IS DEVELOPING THE STRENGTH FOR TOMORROW**

Rating   1   2   3   4   5   Date Used: _____

531.   **THE GIVING OF LOVE IS AN EDUCATION IN ITSELF**
                    — ELEANOR ROOSEVELT

Rating   1   2   3   4   5   Date Used: _____

532.   **DISCIPLINE NOT DESIRE DETERMINE POSITIVE DIRECTION**
                    — CHARLES STANLEY

Rating   1   2   3   4   5   Date Used: _____

533.   **WHAT ONE DOES WHEN NO ONE IS WATCHING SHOWS TRUE CHARACTER**

Rating   1   2   3   4   5   Date Used: _____

534. I HAVE NEVER MET OR HEARD OF ANY ONE WHO COULD OUT SMART HONESTY – ABE LINCOLN

Rating 1 2 3 4 5 Date Used: _____

535. FEAR IS THE TAX THAT CONSCIENCE PAYS TO GUILT
— ZACHARY TAYLOR

Rating 1 2 3 4 5 Date Used: _____

536. FAITH IS A HIGHER FACULTY THAN REASON
— CHARLES TRUBAC

Rating 1 2 3 4 5 Date Used: _____

537. IF HONOR BE YOUR CLOTHING IT WILL LAST A LIFETIME
— GROVER CLEVELAND

Rating 1 2 3 4 5 Date Used: _____

538. ONE MAN WITH COURAGE MAKES A MAJORITY
— ANDREW JACKSON

Rating 1 2 3 4 5 Date Used: _____

539. **ABILITY IS A POOR MAN'S WEALTH — MATTHEW WREN**

Rating   1   2   3   4   5   Date Used: _____

540. **THE BEST TEACHERS OF HUMANITY ARE THE LIVES OF GREAT MEN — FOWLER**

Rating   1   2   3   4   5   Date Used: _____

541. **TO CARRY WORRY TO BED IS TO SLEEP WITH A PACK ON YOUR BACK — HALIBURTON**

Rating   1   2   3   4   5   Date Used: _____

542. **NOTHING SO NEEDS REFORMING AS OTHER PERSONS HABITS — MARK TWAIN**

Rating   1   2   3   4   5   Date Used: _____

543. **A LIGHT HEART LIVES LONGER — SHAKESPEARE**

Rating   1   2   3   4   5   Date Used: _____

544.   MUSIC IS THE
UNIVERSAL LANGUAGE
OF MANKIND
— LONGFELLOW

Rating 1 2 3 4 5 Date Used: _____

545.   MEET SUCCESS LIKE
A GENTLEMAN, DISASTER
LIKE A MAN
— WINSTON CHURCHILL

Rating 1 2 3 4 5 Date Used: _____

546.   EVERY WANTS TO SAVE
THE EARTH BUT NOBODY
WANTS TO HELP MOM
WITH THE DISHES

Rating 1 2 3 4 5 Date Used: _____

547.   THE FEAR OF GOD
MAKES A HERO THE
FEAR OF MAN MAKES
A COWARD

Rating 1 2 3 4 5 Date Used: _____

548.   MOST PEOPLE MISS
OPPORTUNITY BECAUSE IT'S
DRESSED IN OVERHAULS
AND LOOKS LIKE WORK

Rating 1 2 3 4 5 Date Used: _____

549. EMPTY BARRALS MAKE
THE MOST NOISE
— GENERAL JOHN KELLY

Rating 1 2 3 4 5 Date Used: _____

550. NOTHING CAN ECLIPSE
OUR GOD – THANK
HEAVEN

Rating 1 2 3 4 5 Date Used: _____

551. PEOPLE'S INTEGRITY IS
TESTED MOST WHEN
THEY ARE WRONG

Rating 1 2 3 4 5 Date Used: _____

552. A CLEAR CONSCIENCE
IS MORE VALUABLE
THAN WEALTH
— PHILIPPINE PROVERB

Rating 1 2 3 4 5 Date Used: _____

553. WHAT THE LION CAN
NOT DO THE FOX CAN
— GERMAN PROVERB

Rating 1 2 3 4 5 Date Used: _____

554. YOU CHANGE YOUR
LIFE BY CHANGING
YOUR HEART
— MAX LUCADO

Rating 1 2 3 4 5 Date Used: _____

555. TRUST AND INTEGRITY
CAN THRIVE ONLY ON A
FOUNDATION OF
RESPECT AND TRUTH

Rating 1 2 3 4 5 Date Used: _____

556. GOOD DEEDS SOW SEEDS
THOUGH YOU MAY
NOT SEE THE HARVEST

Rating 1 2 3 4 5 Date Used: _____

557. ADVERSITY IS GOD'S
UNIVERSITY
— JOHN HAGEE

Rating 1 2 3 4 5 Date Used: _____

558. GREED ROBS ONE OF
MORE VALUE THAN
THE PRICE OF WHAT
ONE GAINS

Rating 1 2 3 4 5 Date Used: _____

559. **ARROGANCE IS A ROADBLOCK ON THE HIGHWAY OF WISDOM — AMERICAN PROVERB**

Rating 1 2 3 4 5   Date Used: _____

560. **A LOCK IS BETTER THAN SUSPICION — IRISH PROVERB**

Rating 1 2 3 4 5   Date Used: _____

561. **SMALL DEEDS DONE ARE BETTER THAN GREAT DEEDS PLANNED — PETER MARSHALL**

Rating 1 2 3 4 5   Date Used: _____

562. **SAYING THANK YOU IS SPIRITUALLY CORRECT**

Rating 1 2 3 4 5   Date Used: _____

563. **CHRISTIAN GENEROSITY IS NOT MEASURED BY WHAT YOU GIVE BUT BY WHY YOU GIVE**

Rating 1 2 3 4 5   Date Used: _____

564. MAKE YOUR DREAMS GREATER THAN YOUR MEMORIES
— DR. DAVID JEREMIAH

Rating 1 2 3 4 5 Date Used: _____

565. LIVE IN YOUR STRENGTHS LET YOUR WEAKNESSES SHRIVEL UP AND DIE

Rating 1 2 3 4 5 Date Used: _____

566. NO MATTER WHAT THE WEATHER BRING YOUR OWN SUNSHINE

Rating 1 2 3 4 5 Date Used: _____

567. FOR COLLABORATION TO WORK THERE MUST BE TRUST AND OPENNESS

Rating 1 2 3 4 5 Date Used: _____

568. LIFE GETS MORE PRECIOUS WHEN THERE'S LESS OF IT TO WASTE
— BONNIE RAITT

Rating 1 2 3 4 5 Date Used: _____

569. LIFE IS ETERNAL, LOVE IS IMMORTAL, AND DEATH IS A DOORWAY TO BOTH

Rating 1 2 3 4 5 Date Used: _____

570. SILENCE IS OFTEN MISUNDERSTOOD BUT NEVER MISQUOTED

Rating 1 2 3 4 5 Date Used: _____

571. LOVE IS OXYGEN FOR THE SOUL
— DAVID JEREMIAH

Rating 1 2 3 4 5 Date Used: _____

572. LOVE IS WHAT MAKES EVERY OTHER PART OF LIFE MEANINGFUL

Rating 1 2 3 4 5 Date Used: _____

573. JOY IS THE SUREST SIGN OF THE PRESENCE OF GOD
— BRUCE LARSON

Rating 1 2 3 4 5 Date Used: _____

574. THERE ARE NO
SAD SAINTS
— DAVID JEREMIAH

Rating 1   2   3   4   5   Date Used: _____

575. WE CAN'T HAVE THE
JOY OF CHRIST UNTIL
WE HAVE THE CHRIST
OF JOY

Rating 1   2   3   4   5   Date Used: _____

576. PEACE IS NOT THE
ABSENCE OF STRESS
BUT THE PRESENCE
OF JESUS

Rating 1   2   3   4   5   Date Used: _____

577. KNOW CHRIST
KNOW PEACE
NO CHRIST
NO PEACE

Rating 1   2   3   4   5   Date Used: _____

578. INTEGRITY IS TELLING
THE TRUTH TO SELF
HONESTY IS TELLING
THE TRUTH TO OTHERS

Rating 1   2   3   4   5   Date Used: _____

579. **THE LIES WE TELL OURSELVES ARE THE MOST DEADLY**
— DAVID JEREMIAH

Rating 1 2 3 4 5 Date Used: _____

580. **PRIDE IS ALWAYS HUNGRY AND MUST BE FED, HUMILITY IS SELF SUSTAINING**
— DAVID JEREMAIH

Rating 1 2 3 4 5 Date Used: _____

581. **GIVING THE SPIRIT FULL REIGN MAKES FOR A MARVELOUS TRIP**

Rating 1 2 3 4 5 Date Used: _____

582. **GOD IS LORD OF ALL OR HE'S NOT LORD AT ALL**

Rating 1 2 3 4 5 Date Used: _____

583. **FEAR AND IGNORANCE LEAVE WHEN CHARITY AND WISDOM ARRIVE**

Rating 1 2 3 4 5 Date Used: _____

584. ITS GOOD TO BE BLESSED BUT EVEN BETTER TO BE A BLESSING

Rating 1 2 3 4 5 Date Used: _____

585. THE GIFT OF LISTENING CARRIES THE GIFT OF HEALING

Rating 1 2 3 4 5 Date Used: _____

586. FRIENDS INSPIRE YOU OR DRAIN YOU PICK THEM WISELY

Rating 1 2 3 4 5 Date Used: _____

587. DOING RIGHT BRINGS PEACE AND SERENITY DO IT OFTEN

Rating 1 2 3 4 5 Date Used: _____

588. CHRISTMAS IS MORE ABOUT OPENING HEARTS THAN PRESENTS
— JANICE MEADITERE

Rating 1 2 3 4 5 Date Used: _____

589. IN ORDER TO SING MEANINGFUL SONGS YOU MUST LIVE A LIFE OF HARMONY

Rating 1 2 3 4 5 Date Used: _____

590. GOD DOESN'T WANT US IN OUR COMFORT ZONE HE WANTS US IN THE ENDZONE — DAVID JEREMIAH

Rating 1 2 3 4 5 Date Used: _____

591. ITS IMPOSSIBLE TO PROVE THAT GOD DOES NOT EXIST — MICHAEL SAVAGE

Rating 1 2 3 4 5 Date Used: _____

592. THE WISER YOU BECOME THE MORE YOU KNOW WHAT YOU DON'T KNOW

Rating 1 2 3 4 5 Date Used: _____

593. DON'T LET PRAISE OR CRITICISM GET TO YOU THEY CAN BOTH BE HARMFUL

Rating 1 2 3 4 5 Date Used: _____

594. THERE IS NO GREATER
LOAN THAN A
SYMPATHETIC EAR
— FRANK TYGER

Rating 1 2 3 4 5 Date Used: _____

595. TALK TO YOURSELF
LIKE YOU WOULD TO
SOMEONE YOU LOVE
— BRENE BROWN

Rating 1 2 3 4 5 Date Used: _____

596. THE KEY TO WINNING
IS POISE UNDER STRESS
— PAUL BROWN

Rating 1 2 3 4 5 Date Used: _____

597. TO ERR IS HUMAN
TO ADMIT IT VERY
RARE

Rating 1 2 3 4 5 Date Used: _____

598. WHEN WE LEAVE
OURSELVES A WAY OUT
WE USUALLY TAKE IT

Rating 1 2 3 4 5 Date Used: _____

599. **GIVE NOT FROM THE TOP OF YOUR PURSE BUT FROM THE BOTTOM OF YOUR HEART**

Rating 1 2 3 4 5   Date Used: _____

600. **DEEDS ARE FRUIT WORDS ARE LEAVES — ENGLISH PROVERB**

Rating 1 2 3 4 5   Date Used: _____

601. **LYING TO ONESELF IS MORE SERIOUS THAN LYING TO OTHERS**

Rating 1 2 3 4 5   Date Used: _____

602. **AGING LEADS TO WISDOM IF ONE PAYS ATTENTION**

Rating 1 2 3 4 5   Date Used: _____

603. **JUST LOVE EVERYONE I'LL SORT THEM OUT LATER — GOD**

Rating 1 2 3 4 5   Date Used: _____

604. TRUST OTHERS AS YOU WOULD LIKE TO BE TRUSTED

Rating 1 2 3 4 5   Date Used: _____

605. WHEN FAITH AND LOVE SHOW UP FEAR AND ANXIETY LEAVE

Rating 1 2 3 4 5   Date Used: _____

606. OUR ADVERSITY IS GOD'S UNIVERSITY
— JOHN HAGEE

Rating 1 2 3 4 5   Date Used: _____

607. REAL FAITH IS MAN'S WEAKNESS LEANING ON GOD'S STRENGTH
— D.L. MOODY

Rating 1 2 3 4 5   Date Used: _____

608. TOO MUCH RELIGIOUS ACTIVITY IS JUST OLD ADAM IN SUNDAY CLOTHES
— VANCE HAVNER

Rating 1 2 3 4 5   Date Used: _____

609. **THE WAY YOU TELL YOUR STORY TO YOURSELF MATTERS**
— AMY CUDDY

Rating 1 2 3 4 5   Date Used: _____

610. **NOTHING IS HOPELESS THAT IS RIGHT**
— SUSAN B. ANTHONY

Rating 1 2 3 4 5   Date Used: _____

611. **TRUST GOD AND YOURSELF AND YOU WILL KNOW HOW TO LIVE**
— GOETHE

Rating 1 2 3 4 5   Date Used: _____

612. **FEELINGS OF WORTH CAN BEST BE NUTURED IN A LOVING FAMILY**

Rating 1 2 3 4 5   Date Used: _____

613. **YOU ARE THE SOLE AUTHOR OF THE DICTIONARY THAT DEFINES YOU**

Rating 1 2 3 4 5   Date Used: _____

614. **10 LITTLE FINGERS**
10 LITTLE TOES
ON CHRISTMAS HE CAME
ON EASTER HE AROSE

Rating 1 2 3 4 5 Date Used: _____

615. **BE WHO YOU NEEDED**
WHEN YOU WERE
YOUNG

Rating 1 2 3 4 5 Date Used: _____

616. **MAY YOUR CHOICES**
REFLECT YOUR HOPES
NOT YOUR FEARS
— NELSON MANDELA

Rating 1 2 3 4 5 Date Used: _____

617. **IN A WORLD WHERE**
YOU CAN BE ANYTHING
BE KIND

Rating 1 2 3 4 5 Date Used: _____ :

618. **SOMETHING THAT IS**
LOVED IS NEVER LOST
— TONI MORRISON

Rating 1 2 3 4 5 Date Used: _____

619. **TRUE SUCCESS IS OVERCOMING THE FEAR OF BEING UNSUCCESSFUL**
— PAUL SWEENY

Rating 1 2 3 4 5   Date Used: _____

620. **WALK THROUGH LIFE AS IF YOU HAVE SOMETHING TO LEARN, AND YOU WILL**

Rating 1 2 3 4 5   Date Used: _____

621. **RISE ABOVE THE STORM AND YOU WILL FIND THE SUNSHINE**
— MARIO FERNANDEZ

Rating 1 2 3 4 5   Date Used: _____

622. **LIVE LIFE IN CHRIST AS IF IT WILL NEVER END, AND IT WON'T**

Rating 1 2 3 4 5   Date Used: _____

623. **WANTING TO BE MORE LIKE THE MASTER IS WORTHY GOAL**

Rating 1 2 3 4 5   Date Used: _____

624. A TRADITION WITHOUT INTELLIGENCE IS NOT WORTH HAVING

Rating 1 2 3 4 5 Date Used: _____

625. FAITH IS A SPIRITUAL RESURRECTION OF THE SOUL
— JOHN CALVIN

Rating 1 2 3 4 5 Date Used: _____

626. THE BIBLE IS GOD'S LIVING WORD, READ, LISTEN, AND GOD WILL SPEAK TO YOU

Rating 1 2 3 4 5 Date Used: _____

627. WORK AS IF YOU WERE TO LIVE TO BE 100, PRAY AS IF YOU WOULD DIE TOMORROW — BEN FRANKLIN

Rating 1 2 3 4 5 Date Used: _____

628. WHEN YOU INCURR DEBT YOU GIVE ANOTHER POWER OVER YOUR LIBERTY
— BEN FRANKLIN

Rating 1 2 3 4 5 Date Used: _____

629. IF THE WIND WILL
NOT SERVE TAKE
TO THE OARS
— LATIN PROVERB

Rating 1 2 3 4 5   Date Used: _____

630. UNKIND PEOPLE NEED
YOUR LOVE THE MOST
THEY ADVERTISE
THEIR PAIN

Rating 1 2 3 4 5   Date Used: _____

631. A MOTHER'S LOVE IS
SPECIAL, BUT ONLY A
SAMPLE OF GOD'S
GREATER LOVE FOR US

Rating 1 2 3 4 5   Date Used: _____

632. ANYONE WHO TRIES TO
PULL YOU DOWN IS
ALREADY BELOW YOU

Rating 1 2 3 4 5   Date Used: _____

633. LIFE IS SHORT EAT
THE DESSERT FIRST
— JACQUES TORRES

Rating 1 2 3 4 5   Date Used: _____

634. BE A RAINBOW IN SOMEONE ELSE'S RAINSTORM

Rating 1 2 3 4 5 Date Used: _____

635. NOT ALL CAN DO GREAT THINGS BUT WE CAN ALL DO THINGS WITH GREAT LOVE — MOTHER TERESA

Rating 1 2 3 4 5 Date Used: _____

634. PREFER TO BELIEVE THE BEST OF EVERYONE IT SAVES MUCH TROUBLE — RUDYARD KIPLING

Rating 1 2 3 4 5 Date Used: _____

635. EVERYONE IS FIGHTING A BATTLE YOU KNOW NOTHING ABOUT – BE KIND

Rating 1 2 3 4 5 Date Used: _____

636. LAZINESS MAY APPEAR ATTRACTIVE BUT IT DESTROYS SELF-WORTH

Rating 1 2 3 4 5 Date Used: _____

637. **JUDGE YOUR WORDS BY:
IS IT TRUE? IS IT KIND?
IS IT NECESSARY?**

Rating   1   2   3   4   5   Date Used: _____

638. **ANGER, HURT, AND PAIN
CAN STEAL ENERGY AND
UNDERMINE LOVE**

Rating   1   2   3   4   5   Date Used: _____

639. **TIE UP YOUR LOOSE
ENDS TO NOT KNOT
CAN BE HARMFUL**

Rating   1   2   3   4   5   Date Used: _____

640. **PEACE IS ALWAYS
BEAUTIFUL
— WALT WHITMAN**

Rating   1   2   3   4   5   Date Used: _____

641. **OUR ATTENTION IS
A CURRENCY SPEND
IT WISELY**

Rating   1   2   3   4   5   Date Used: _____

642. HUMOR CAN BE A MAJOR TOOL FOR INSIGHT CHANGING "HA – HA" TO "AHA"

Rating 1 2 3 4 5   Date Used: _____

643. LONELINESS CAN BE CONQUERED ONLY BY THOSE WHO CAN BEAR SOLITUDE — P. TILLICH

Rating 1 2 3 4 5   Date Used: _____

644. THE TRUTH IS HARD TO SWALLOW WHEN YOU'RE CHOKING ON YOUR PRIDE — MEAT LOAF

Rating 1 2 3 4 5   Date Used: _____

645. THOSE WHO SAY SOMETHING CAN'T BE DONE SHOULD NOT STOP THOSE DOING IT

Rating 1 2 3 4 5   Date Used: _____

646. MORALS ARE HABITS OF A HEART FOCUSED ON GOD — ANONYMOUS

Rating 1 2 3 4 5   Date Used: _____

647. CHRISTIANS NEVER SAY GOOD-BYE, JUST "UNTIL WE MEET AGAIN"
—WOODROW KROLL

Rating 1 2 3 4 5 Date Used: _____

648. THINK FOR YOURSELF AND LET OTHERS ENJOY THE PRIVILEGE TOO.
— VOLTAIRE

Rating 1 2 3 4 5 Date Used: _____

649. ONE OF THE KEYS TO HAPPINESS IS A BAD MEMORY
— RITA MAE BROWN

Rating 1 2 3 4 5 Date Used: _____

650. ANGER IS A FEELING THAT MAKES YOUR MOUTH WORK FASTER THAN YOUR MIND
— EVAN ESAR

Rating 1 2 3 4 5 Date Used: _____

651. IT TAKES TWO TO TANGO OR FIGHT IT'S BETTER TO DANCE

Rating 1 2 3 4 5 Date Used: _____

652. THE ESSENCE OF FAITH
LIES IN THE HEART'S
CHOICE OF CHRIST
— CHARLES SPURGEON

Rating 1 2 3 4 5   Date Used: _____

653. ONE MAN WITH GOD
ON HIS SIDE IS ALWAYS
IN THE MAJORITY
— JOHN KNOX

Rating 1 2 3 4 5   Date Used: _____

654. THE LORD'S GOODNESS
SURROUNDS US AT
EVERY MOMENT
— R.W. BARBOUR

Rating 1 2 3 4 5   Date Used: _____

655. THE ROAD TO SUCCESS
IS ALWAYS UNDER
CONSTRUCTION
— LILY TOMLIN

Rating 1 2 3 4 5   Date Used: _____

656. PERPETUAL OPTIMISM
IS A FORCE MULTIPLIER
— COLIN POWELL

Rating 1 2 3 4 5   Date Used: _____

657.   **ITS BETTER TO FLIRT WITH FAILURE THAN TO NEVER KNOW SUCCESS**

Rating   1   2   3   4   5   Date Used: _____

658.   **A WISE MAN CHANGES HIS MIND; A FOOL NEVER WILL**
        — SPANISH PROVERB

Rating   1   2   3   4   5   Date Used: _____

659.   **GOD DOESN'T CALL THE EQUIPED HE EQUIPS THE CALLED**
        — DAVID JEREMIAH

Rating   1   2   3   4   5   Date Used: _____

660.   **IS LIFE A PUZZLE? GOD HAS THE MISSING PEACE**

Rating   1   2   3   4   5   Date Used: _____

661.   **THREE THINGS TELL A PERSON: THEIR EYES, THEIR FRIENDS, AND THEIR FAVORITE QUOTES**

Rating   1   2   3   4   5   Date Used: _____

652.   BELIEVING TAKES PRACTICE
— MADELINE L'ENGLE

Rating   1   2   3   4   5   Date Used: _____

653.   IT TAKES STRENGTH TO BE GENTLE AND KIND
— STEVEN MORRISSEY

Rating   1   2   3   4   5   Date Used: _____

654.   LOVE IS THE POWER TO SEE SIMILARITY IN DISSIMILARITY
— THEODORE ADORNO

Rating   1   2   3   4   5   Date Used: _____

655.   TO EASE ANOTHER'S BURDEN HELP CARRY IT
— HENRI BERGSON

Rating   1   2   3   4   5   Date Used: _____

656.   REAL LOVE IS A PERMANENTLY SELF-ENLARGING EXPERIENCE
— M. SCOTT PECK

Rating   1   2   3   4   5   Date Used: _____

657. **BOLDLY VENTURED IS HALF WON**
— GERMAN PROVERB

Rating 1 2 3 4 5 Date Used: _____

658. **SPEAK THE TRUTH ALWAYS ESPECIALLY TO YOURSELF**

Rating 1 2 3 4 5 Date Used: _____

659. **WHEN PASSIONS ARE MOST INFLAMED FAIRNESS IS MOST IN JEOPARDY**
— SEN. SUSAN COLLINS

Rating 1 2 3 4 5 Date Used: _____

660. **ACRONYM FOR CHAOS: CHRIST HAS ALL OUR SOLUTIONS**

Rating 1 2 3 4 5 Date Used: _____

661. **IF YOUR BIBLE IS FALLING APART IT MEANS YOU ARE NOT**

Rating 1 2 3 4 5 Date Used: _____

662. **JOY IS THE SERIOUS BUSINESS OF HEAVEN**
— C.S. LEWIS

Rating 1 2 3 4 5 Date Used: _____

663. SATAN TEMPTS US
TO MAKE US WORSE
GOD TESTS US TO
MAKE US BETTER

Rating 1 2 3 4 5   Date Used: _____

664. MISTAKES DO NOT
DEFINE CHRISTIANS
IT'S HOW THEY
MAKE AMENDS

Rating 1 2 3 4 5   Date Used: _____

665. ONE'S SPEED IS LESS
IMPORTANT THAN
ONE'S DIRECTION

Rating 1 2 3 4 5   Date Used: _____

666. THE HEART THAT
GIVES, GATHERS
—MARIANNE MOORE

Rating 1 2 3 4 5   Date Used: _____

667. MAKE YOUR BREAKING
POINT YOUR TURNING
POINT
— DENNIS KIMBO

Rating 1 2 3 4 5   Date Used: _____

668. WE CANNOT LOVE
OTHERS IF WE DONOT
LOVE OURSELVES

Rating 1 2 3 4 5 Date Used: _____

669. AWARDING MEDIOCRATY
IS REWARDING LOSING

Rating 1 2 3 4 5 Date Used: _____

670. NOTHING IS MORE TRULY
ARTISTIC THAN TO
LOVE PEOPLE
— VINCENT VAN GOGH

Rating 1 2 3 4 5 Date Used: _____

671. HUMOR IS THE
UNIVERSAL SOLVENT
FOR THE ABRASIVENESS
OF LIFE

Rating 1 2 3 4 5 Date Used: _____

672. CARISMA IS MAKING
OTHERS LIKE YOU
WITHOUT KNOWING
WHY

Rating 1 2 3 4 5 Date Used: _____

673. GRACE IS BUT GLORY BEGUN, GLORY IS BUT GRACE PERFECTED

Rating 1 2 3 4 5 Date Used: _____

674. ONE NEGLECT OFTEN LEADS TO SEVERAL REGRETS

Rating 1 2 3 4 5 Date Used: _____

675. WHY DO ANYTHING OTHER THAN GOOD? IT PAYS THE BEST DIVIDENDS

Rating 1 2 3 4 5 Date Used: _____

676. WHEREVER YOU GO BRING YOUR OWN SUNSHINE

Rating 1 2 3 4 5 Date Used: _____

677. CHRISTMAS IS THE DAY THAT HOLDS ALL TIME TOGETHER
— ALEXANDER SMITH

Rating 1 2 3 4 5 Date Used: _____

678. THE BEST CHRISTMAS PRESENTS WE CAN GIVE EACH OTHER ARE LOVE AND JOY

Rating 1 2 3 4 5 Date Used: _____

679. A MISTAKE ISN'T A MISTAKE UNLESS IT CAN'T BE CORRECTED

Rating 1 2 3 4 5 Date Used: _____

680. FOLLOW THE ADVICE OF TREES: IN WINTER THEY SHED THE UNNECESSARY AND STAY FULLY ROOTED

Rating 1 2 3 4 5 Date Used: _____

681. WISDOM IS DOING THE RIGHT THING AND KNOWING WHY

Rating 1 2 3 4 5 Date Used: _____

682. EXPERIENCE TEACHES ONLY THE TEACHEABLE
—ALDOUS HUXLEY

Rating 1 2 3 4 5 Date Used: _____

683. YOU CANNOT FIND PEACE
BY AVOIDING LIFE
— VIRGINIA WOOLF

Rating 1 2 3 4 5   Date Used: _____

684. DO NOT TALK TO
YOURSELF UNLESS YOU
INTEND TO LISTEN

Rating 1 2 3 4 5   Date Used: _____

685. IF GOD DOESN'T GUIDE
YOU SATAN AND
EVIL WILL

Rating 1 2 3 4 5   Date Used: _____

686. OUR GIVING TO GOD
IS A MEASURE OF
OUR TRUST IN HIM

Rating 1 2 3 4 5   Date Used: _____

687. WHAT EVER MOVES
THE HEART WAGS
THE TONGUE
— C.T. STUDD

Rating 1 2 3 4 5   Date Used: _____

688. THE KEY TO GODLINESS
IS NOT MORE KNOWLEDGE
IT'S MORE OBEDIENCE
— WOODROW KROLL

Rating 1 2 3 4 5 Date Used: _____

689. HOT HEADS AND COLD
HEARTS NEVER
SOLVED ANYTHING
— BILLY GRAHAM

Rating 1 2 3 4 5 Date Used: _____

690. IT IS BETTER TO GET
WISDOM THAN GOLD
— MATTHEW HENRY

Rating 1 2 3 4 5 Date Used: _____

691. IT'S EASIER TO LOVE
SOMEONE IF YOU DON'T
EXPECT THEM TO BE
PERFECT

Rating 1 2 3 4 5 Date Used: _____

692. DON'T HELP OTHERS
FEEL INSECURE THEY
USUALLY HAVE MORE
HELP THAN NEEDED

Rating 1 2 3 4 5 Date Used: _____

693. WITHOUT A SONG EACH DAY WOULD BE A CENTURY
— MAHALIA JACKSON

Rating 1 2 3 4 5 Date Used: _____

694. TIME FLIES WASTING IT KILLS SUCCESS

Rating 1 2 3 4 5 Date Used: _____

695. LAZINESS IS NOTHING MORE THAN RESTING BEFORE YOU GET TIRED
— JULES RENARD

Rating 1 2 3 4 5 Date Used: _____

696. TAKE THE HIGH ROAD THERE'S A TRAFFIC JAM ON THE LOW ROAD

Rating 1 2 3 4 5 Date Used: _____

697. PERSERVERANCE IS A GREAT SUBSTITUTE FOR TALENT
— STEVE MARTIN

Rating 1 2 3 4 5 Date Used: _____

698. **WHAT PEOPLE FIND MOST IRRITATING IN OTHERS ARE THEIR OWN FAULTS**

Rating   1   2   3   4   5   Date Used: _____

699. **GRACE CAN ONLY GROW OUT OF HUMILITY**

Rating   1   2   3   4   5   Date Used: _____

700. **BEWARE OF REASONING ABOUT GOD'S WORD -- OBEY IT!**
— OSWALD CHAMBERS

Rating   1   2   3   4   5   Date Used: _____

701. **CHRIST IS OUR TEMPLE IN WHOM BY FAITH ALL BELIEVERS MEET**
— MATTHEW HENRY

Rating   1   2   3   4   5   Date Used: _____

702. **THE MORE TERRIBLE THE STORM THE MORE NECESSARY THE ANCHOR**
— WILLIAM PLUMER

Rating   1   2   3   4   5   Date Used: _____

703. THE TAKING AWAY OF
GOD, EVEN IN THOUGHT,
DISSOLVES ALL
— JOHN LOCKE

Rating   1   2   3   4   5   Date Used: _____

704. FAITH IS LIKE LOVE
WHEN WE HOARD IT
IT SHRIVELS

Rating   1   2   3   4   5   Date Used: _____

705. ONLY A VIRTUOUS
PEOPLE ARE CAPABLE
OF FREEDOM
— BEN FRANKLIN

Rating   1   2   3   4   5   Date Used: _____

706. NO AMOUNT OF MONEY
CAN COERCE VIRTUE

Rating   1   2   3   4   5   Date Used: _____

707. THE SAFEST ROAD TO
HELL IS THE SOFT
GRADUAL ONE

Rating   1   2   3   4   5   Date Used: _____

708. **HAPPINESS IS LESS GETTING WHAT WE WANT THAN WANTING WHAT WE HAVE**

Rating 1 2 3 4 5 Date Used: _____

709. **LOVE IS NO LOVE THAT ASKS FOR A RETURN — M. GANDHI**

Rating 1 2 3 4 5 Date Used: _____

710. **POWER COMES FROM 2 SOURCES: FORCE AND LOVE. THE LATTER IS BEST**

Rating 1 2 3 4 5 Date Used: _____

711. **TO VIEW A BEAUTIFUL ORCHID AND BELIEVE IN EVOLUTION REQUIRES AN AMAZING IGNORANCE**

Rating 1 2 3 4 5 Date Used: _____

712. **AS THE EARTH COMES ALIVE IN SPRING WE ARE REMINDED OF ITS INTELLIGENT DESIGNER**

Rating 1 2 3 4 5 Date Used: _____

713. NO ONE IS TOO OLD
TO LEARN
— GERMAN PROVERB

Rating 1 2 3 4 5 Date Used: _____

714. DEAL WITH THE FAULTS
OF OTHERS AS GENTLY
AS YOUR OWN

Rating 1 2 3 4 5 Date Used: _____

715. PEOPLE START TO HEAL
AS SOON AS THEY
FEEL HEARD
— CHERYL RICHARDSON

Rating 1 2 3 4 5 Date Used: _____

716. ARROGANCE IS AN
UNHEALTHY EGO IN
NEED OF REPAIR
— THOMAS FARANDA

Rating 1 2 3 4 5 Date Used: _____

717. IF YOU ARE AFRAID OF
BEING LONELY DON'T
TRY TO BE RIGHT
— JULES RENARD

Rating 1 2 3 4 5 Date Used: _____

718. ANGER IS THE WIND THAT BLOWS OUT THE LAMP OF THE MIND
— ROBERT INGERSOLL

Rating 1 2 3 4 5 Date Used: _____

719. THE MORE TERRIBLE THE STORM THE MORE NECESSARY THE ANCHOR
— WM. PLUMER

Rating 1 2 3 4 5 Date Used: _____

720. GOD'S PEOPLE MAY GROAN BUT THEY DO NOT GRUMBLE
— CHARLES SPURGEON

Rating 1 2 3 4 5 Date Used: _____

721. DO YOUR BEST WHEN NO ONE ELSE IS LOOKING ONLY GOD WILL SEE

Rating 1 2 3 4 5 Date Used: _____

722. NOTHING HAS MORE STRENGTH THAN DIRE NECESSITY
— EURIPIDES

Rating 1 2 3 4 5 Date Used: _____

723. CONSERVATION IS A
STATE OF HARMONY
BETWEEN HUMANS
GOD AND NATURE

Rating 1 2 3 4 5   Date Used: _____

724. A BAD ATTITUDE IS
LIKE A FLAT TIRE
YOU MUST CHANGE
IT TO GO FORWARD

Rating 1 2 3 4 5   Date Used: _____

725. DEATH DIED WHEN
CHRIST AROSE

Rating 1 2 3 4 5   Date Used: _____

726. WHEN WE ARE DOWN
TO NOTHING GOD IS
UP TO SOMETHING
— JOHN HAGEE

Rating 1 2 3 4 5   Date Used: _____

727. ANYONE WHO HAS NOT
MET SATAN HEAD-ON
MAY BE GOING IN THE
SAME DIRECTION

Rating 1 2 3 4 5   Date Used: _____

728. IF GOD IS IN A CAUSE IT CAN'T BE BAD AND FAILURE WILL BE HARD

Rating 1 2 3 4 5 Date Used: _____

729. HERE IS A FACT: REBUILDERS NEVER CUT WHAT THEY CAN UNTIE

Rating 1 2 3 4 5 Date Used: _____

730. GIVING IN ON A NON-ESSENTIAL IS OKAY ON AN ESSENTIAL IT IS NOT

Rating 1 2 3 4 5 Date Used: _____

731. HISTORY SHOWS THAT ALL GREAT NATIONS COMMIT SUICIDE — ARNOLD TOYNBEE

Rating 1 2 3 4 5 Date Used: _____

732. FOLLOW A "YOU CAN'T DO IT" WITH A "WATCH ME"

Rating 1 2 3 4 5 Date Used: _____

733. TO SUCCEED FIND
YOUR POTENTIAL
THEN BLOW PAST IT

Rating 1 2 3 4 5 Date Used: _____

734. HELPING BEGINS
WITH LISTENING
— GLORIA STEINEM

Rating 1 2 3 4 5 Date Used: _____

735. THE GREATER THE
LIGHT WITHIN YOU
THE BRIGHTER THE
WORLD WILL BE

Rating 1 2 3 4 5 Date Used: _____

736. CELEBRATE UNITY
NOT DIVERSITY

Rating 1 2 3 4 5 Date Used: _____

737. THE BEST OF ALL
IS GOD WITH US
— JOHN WESLEY

Rating 1 2 3 4 5 Date Used: _____

738. THE HIGHEST HONOR IN
THE CHURCH IS NOT
GOVERNMENT BUT
SERVICE — J. CALVIN

Rating 1 2 3 4 5 Date Used: _____

739. IN CREATION WE SEE
GOD'S WISDOM ON
FULL DISPLAY

Rating 1 2 3 4 5 Date Used: _____

740. LOVE RECOGNIZES
NO BARRIERS
— MAYA ANGELO

Rating 1 2 3 4 5 Date Used: _____

741. YOU CAN'T STOP THE
WAVES BUT YOU CAN
LEARN TO SURF

Rating 1 2 3 4 5 Date Used: _____

742. AT THE GATES OF
PATIENCE THERE IS
NO CROWDING

Rating 1 2 3 4 5 Date Used: _____

743. LIFE WITH GOD IS
MARVELOUS AND WHEN
IT ENDS IT GETS
EVEN BETTER

Rating 1 2 3 4 5 Date Used: _____

744. DIVERSITY DIVIDES
UNITY HARMONIZES

Rating 1 2 3 4 5 Date Used: _____

745. CELEBRATE UNITY
NOT DIVERSITY

Rating 1 2 3 4 5 Date Used: _____

746. A FATHER'S HOLY LIFE
IS A RICH LEGACY
FOR HIS SONS
— CHARLES SPURGEON

Rating 1 2 3 4 5 Date Used: _____

747. FAITH IS GOD
FELT BY THE HEART
— PASCAL

Rating 1 2 3 4 5 Date Used: _____

748. WHEN SATAN DEPLORES
US AND THE WORLD
IGNORES US GOD
RESTORES US

Rating 1 2 3 4 5 Date Used: _____

749. FRIENDSHIP IS THE
MARRIAGE OF
AFFECTIONS

Rating 1 2 3 4 5 Date Used: _____

750. YOU CANNOT LOVE A THING WITHOUT WANTING TO FIGHT FOR IT
— G.K. CHESTERTON

Rating 1 2 3 4 5 Date Used: _____

751. MUDDY WATER IS BEST CLEARED BY LEAVING IT ALONE
— ALAN WATTS

Rating 1 2 3 4 5 Date Used: _____

752. A FEAR GREATER THAN FAILURE IS SUCCEEDING AT THINGS THAT DON'T MATTER

Rating 1 2 3 4 5 Date Used: _____

753. IF YOU'RE GOING IN THE WRONG DIRECTION REMEMBER LIFE PERMITS U TURNS

Rating 1 2 3 4 5 Date Used: _____

754. WORRY IS PRACTICAL ATHEISM
— JOHN HAGEE

Rating 1 2 3 4 5 Date Used: _____

755. USE YOUR FREEDOM
TO CHOOSE NOT
WHAT YOUR PAST
IMPOSES ON YOU

Rating 1 2 3 4 5 Date Used: _____

756. WORK HARDER ON
YOURSELF THAN
YOU DO ON YOUR
FRIENDS

Rating 1 2 3 4 5 Date Used: _____

757. YOUR DREAMS CAN BE
A PREVIEW OF COMING
ATTRACTIONS

Rating 1 2 3 4 5 Date Used: _____

758. BEHAVIOR IS A MIRROR
IN WHICH WE SEE OUR
OWN IMAGE

Rating 1 2 3 4 5 Date Used: _____

759. NEVER BE ASHAMED
OF THE SUFFERING
YOU'VE BEEN THROUGH

Rating 1 2 3 4 5 Date Used: _____

760. AN ESSENTIAL IN LIFE IS A CLEAR UNDERSTANDING OF ONE'S WORLDVIEW

Rating 1 2 3 4 5 Date Used: _____

761. ONE ADVANTAGE OF TALKING TO YOURSELF IS YOU MAY BE LISTENING

Rating 1 2 3 4 5 Date Used: _____

762. FERTILIZER STINKS BUT IT MAKES THINGS GROW, SO DOES FAILURE

Rating 1 2 3 4 5 Date Used: _____

763. THERE ARE ONLY TWO RACES THE DECENT AND THE INDECENT — VIKTOR FRANKL

Rating 1 2 3 4 5 Date Used: _____

764. LIVE TO THE HILT EVERY SITUATION YOU BELIEVE IS THE WILL OF GOD – JIM ELLIOT

Rating 1 2 3 4 5 Date Used: _____

765. EVERY TEAR OF SORROW SOWN BY THE RIGHTEOUS SPRINGS UP A PEARL
— MATHEW HENRY

Rating 1 2 3 4 5 Date Used: _____

766. GAIN ALL YOU CAN SAVE ALL YOU CAN THEN GIVE ALL YOU CAN
— JOHN WESLEY

Rating 1 2 3 4 5 Date Used: _____

767. NO TEMPTATION IS MORE BEFORE US THAN EASING UP
— SINCLAIR FERGUSON

Rating 1 2 3 4 5 Date Used: _____

768. AFFLICTION IS GOOD IF IT TEACHES US HOW TO HELP OTHERS IN DISTRESS

Rating 1 2 3 4 5 Date Used: _____

769. THERE ARE NONE MORE BLIND THAN THOSE WHO CANNOT SEE GOD'S TRUTH

Rating 1 2 3 4 5 Date Used: _____

770. **FOLLOW GOD'S WILL AND WHAT LOOKS LIKE WALLS WILL TURN INTO DOORS**

Rating 1 2 3 4 5 Date Used: _____

771. **PROBLEMS ARE NOT STOP SIGNS THEY ARE GUIDELINES — ROBERT SCHULLER**

Rating 1 2 3 4 5 Date Used: _____

772. **IT IS BEST TO LIVE LIFE FULLER RATHER THAN FASTER**

Rating 1 2 3 4 5 Date Used: _____

773. **MAKING A DIFFERENCE AND MAKING MONEY ARE NOT THE SAME**

Rating 1 2 3 4 5 Date Used: _____

774. **UNPLUGGING A COMPUTER FOR A SHORT TIME OFTEN HELPS IT RUN BETTER, ITS THE SAME FOR PEOPLE**

Rating 1 2 3 4 5 Date Used: _____

775. ANYONE CAN GET A
PH. D IN LOVING

Rating 1 2 3 4 5 Date Used: _____

776. A PENNY SAVED IS
A GOVERNMENT
OVERSIGHT

Rating 1 2 3 4 5 Date Used: _____

777. WHEN DEALING WITH
YOURSELF USE YOUR HEAD
WHEN DEALING WITH
OTHERS USE YOUR HEART

Rating 1 2 3 4 5 Date Used: _____

778. HOLINESS IN THE SEED
SHALL HAVE HAPPINESS
IN THE HARVEST

Rating 1 2 3 4 5 Date Used: _____

779. DON'T LET PEOPLE
DRIVE YOU CRAZY
WHEN YOU CAN
EASILY WALK THERE

Rating 1 2 3 4 5 Date Used: _____

780. DON'T BURN YOUR BRIDGES UNTIL AFTER YOU HAVE CROSSED OVER

Rating 1 2 3 4 5 Date Used: _____

781. OF TWO EVILS CHOOSE NEITHER
— CHARLES SPURGEON

Rating 1 2 3 4 5 Date Used: _____

782. MAN IS MOST FREE WHEN CONTROLLED BY GOD ALONE
— AUGUSTINE

Rating 1 2 3 4 5 Date Used: _____

783. FRIENDSHIP FLOURSIHES AT THE FOUNTAIN OF FORGIVENESS
— WM. WARD

Rating 1 2 3 4 5 Date Used: _____

784. IT'S BETTER TO WALK WITH GOD IN THE DARK THEN TO WALK ALONE IN THE LIGHT

Rating 1 2 3 4 5 Date Used: _____

785. WHEN LIFE GETS TOO
HARD TO STAND
KNEEL BEFORE GOD

Rating 1 2 3 4 5   Date Used: _____

786. GRATITUDE TURNS WHAT
WE HAVE INTO ENOUGH

Rating 1 2 3 4 5   Date Used: _____

787. ALL WE NEED EACH
DAY IS A LITTLE BIT
OF COFFEE AND A
WHOLE LOT OF JESUS

Rating 1 2 3 4 5   Date Used: _____

788. JESUS: HE CAME
FOR YOU
MERRY CHRISTMAS

Rating 1 2 3 4 5   Date Used: _____

789. DANGER IS REAL
BUT FEAR IS A
CHOICE

Rating 1 2 3 4 5   Date Used: _____

790. **GIVE CHEERFULLY ACCEPT GRATEFULLY AND EVERYONE IS BLESSED – MAYA ANGELO**

Rating 1 2 3 4 5 Date Used: _____

791. **PEOPLE WHO THROW KISSES ARE HOPELESSLY LAZY — BOB HOPE**

Rating 1 2 3 4 5 Date Used: _____

792. **THE LANGUAGE OF FRIENDSHIP IS NOT WORDS BUT MEANINGS — HENRY D. THOREAU**

Rating 1 2 3 4 5 Date Used: _____

793. **GUILT KEEPS PEOPLE IMPRISONED IN THEMSELVES — IRIS MURDOCH**

Rating 1 2 3 4 5 Date Used: _____

794. **UNTIL GOD OPENS THE NEXT DOOR PRAISE HIM IN THE HALLWAY**

Rating 1 2 3 4 5 Date Used: _____

795. JOY IS DELIGHT IN GOD'S GRACE WHICH ENABLES US TO ENDURE OUR TRIALS
— GEORGE SEEVERS

Rating 1 2 3 4 5 Date Used: _____

796. THE WAY TO COVER OUR SIN IS TO UNCOVER IT BY CONFESSION
— RICHARD SIBBES

Rating 1 2 3 4 5 Date Used: _____

797. YANK SOME OF THE GROANS OUT OF YOUR PRAYERS AND SHOVE IN SOME SHOUTS — B. SUNDAY

Rating 1 2 3 4 5 Date Used: _____

798. NO MAN EVER REPENTED FOR BEING A CHRISTIAN ON HIS DEATH BED
— HANNAH MORE

Rating 1 2 3 4 5 Date Used: _____

799. WORRY AND WORSHIP ARE MUTUALLY EXCLUSIVE

Rating 1 2 3 4 5 Date Used: _____

800. LOVE IS THE POWER
BEHIND CHRISTMAS
RECEIVE IT - SHARE IT

Rating 1 2 3 4 5 Date Used: _____

801. CRIME WOULD NEVER
PAY IF THE GOVERNMENT
RAN IT

Rating 1 2 3 4 5 Date Used: _____

802. IF YOU WANT LIGHT
IN YOUR LIFE STAND
WHERE THE SON IS
SHINING

Rating 1 2 3 4 5 Date Used: _____

803. MANY THINGS HAVE
GREAT BEAUTY BUT
NOT ALL SEE IT

Rating 1 2 3 4 5 Date Used: _____

804. EMPATHY GROWS AS
WE DEVELOP SYMPATHY
FOR OTHERS

Rating 1 2 3 4 5 Date Used: _____

805.   LOVE IS MORE
IMPORTANT THAN GOLD
CHRISTMAS TEACHES
THAT TRUTH

Rating 1   2   3   4   5   Date Used: _____

806.   PEOPLE SEE WHAT
WE DO GOD SEES
WHY WE DO IT

Rating 1   2   3   4   5   Date Used: _____

807.   LOVE BEGINS WHEN WE
VALUE SOMEONE MORE
THEN OURSELVES
THAT'S A MOTHER'S LOVE

Rating 1   2   3   4   5   Date Used: _____

808.   BE HUMBLE. PERSERVERE.
READ MORE. TOUGHEN UP.
— TAI LOPEZ

Rating 1   2   3   4   5   Date Used: _____

809.   KNOWING WHAT IS
IMPORTANT CLARIFIES
WHAT IS NOT

Rating 1   2   3   4   5   Date Used: _____

810. DON'T NEGLECT THE
GOLD IN YOUR
BACKYARD
— BEN OKRI

Rating 1 2 3 4 5 Date Used: _____

811. I DECIDED TO STAY WITH
LOVE, HATE IS TOO HEAVY
A BURDEN TO BEAR
— MARTIN L. KING

Rating 1 2 3 4 5 Date Used: _____

812. FEW MEN HAVE VIRTUE
TO WITHSTAND THE
HIGHEST BIDDER
— GEORGE WASHINTON

Rating 1 2 3 4 5 Date Used: _____

813. A PEOPLE THAT ELECT
CORRUPT POLITICIANS
ARE NOT VICTIMS BUT
ACCOMPLICIES — G. ORWELL

Rating 1 2 3 4 5 Date Used: _____

814. THE MAN WHO REMOVES
A MOUNTAIN BEGINS BY
CARRYING SMALL STONES
— WILLIAM FAULKNER

Rating 1 2 3 4 5 Date Used: _____

815. YOU CAN TELL WHEN YOU ARE ON THE ROAD TO SUCCESS; ITS UPHILL ALL THE WAY – PAUL HARVEY

Rating 1 2 3 4 5 Date Used: _____

816. BOREDOM IS THE RESULT OF FAILING TO ACTIVATE UNUSED CAPABILITIES

Rating 1 2 3 4 5 Date Used: _____

817. LIFE AND TIME ARE TOO SHORT SPEAK WORDS THAT MATTER

Rating 1 2 3 4 5 Date Used: _____

818. GO WHERE THE SILENCE IS AND SAY SOMETHING — AMY GOODMAN

Rating 1 2 3 4 5 Date Used: _____

819. CONSCIENCE IS THE PERFECT INTERPRETER OF LIFE — KARL BARTH

Rating 1 2 3 4 5 Date Used: _____

820. GREET OTHERS WITH A SMILE FOR IT IS THE BEGINNING OF LOVE
— MOTHER TERESA

Rating 1 2 3 4 5 Date Used: _____

821. VALUE RELATIONSHIPS MORE THAN POSESSIONS
— ANTHONY J. D'ANGELO

Rating 1 2 3 4 5 Date Used: _____

822. NOTHING IN FINE PRINT IS EVER GOOD NEWS
— ANDY ROONEY

Rating 1 2 3 4 5 Date Used: _____

823. LIFE IS LIKE A BOWL OF SPAGHETTI NOW AND THEN YOU FIND A MEATBALL

Rating 1 2 3 4 5 Date Used: _____

824. EVEN IF WE'RE NOT THE SHARPEST CRAYON IN THE BOX WE CAN STILL BRING SOME COLOR TO OTHERS

Rating 1 2 3 4 5 Date Used: _____

825. THE FEAR OF GOD
CAN DELIVER US FROM
THE FEAR OF MAN
— JOHN WITHERSPOON

Rating 1 2 3 4 5   Date Used: _____

826. GOSSIP IS THE ART OF
CONFESSING OTHER
PEOPLE'S SINS

Rating 1 2 3 4 5   Date Used: _____

827. NEVER BE AFRAID TO
TRUST AN UNKNOWN
FUTURE TO A KNOWN GOD
— CORRIE TEN BOOM

Rating 1 2 3 4 5   Date Used: _____

828. FEAR HAS ONLY AS
MUCH POWER AS WE
GIVE IT SPACE
— JOHN RITTER

Rating 1 2 3 4 5   Date Used: _____

829. PRAISE IS A VALUABLE
ASSET IF NOT AIMED
AT ONESELF

Rating 1 2 3 4 5   Date Used: _____

830. WAITING TO DO SOMETHING IMPORTANT ONLY MAKES ONE OLDER

Rating 1 2 3 4 5 Date Used: _____

831. WITHOUT MORAL COURAGE ALL VIRTUE IS MERELY A WAY OF SPEAKING
— MORDECAI KAPLAN

Rating 1 2 3 4 5 Date Used: _____

832. A SMILE IS FREE GIVE IT AWAY NOW AND ALL WILL SEE AND ALSO KNOW HOW

Rating 1 2 3 4 5 Date Used: _____

833. IF THERE IS NO GOD EVERYTHING IS PERMITTED
— F. DOSTOYEVSKY

Rating 1 2 3 4 5 Date Used: _____

834. IF MAN IS NOT GOVERNED BY GOD HE WILL BE RULED BY TYRANTS

Rating 1 2 3 4 5 Date Used: _____

835.   **EXPERTS MADE THE TITANIC AMATEURS MADE THE ARK**

Rating 1 2 3 4 5 Date Used: _____

836.   **I HATE THIS CHURCH — SATAN**

Rating 1 2 3 4 5 Date Used: _____

837.   **TOO COLD TO CHANGE SIGN – MESSAGE INSIDE**

Rating 1 2 3 4 5 Date Used: _____

838.   **IF LIFE STINKS, WE HAVE A PEW INSIDE**

Rating 1 2 3 4 5 Date Used: _____

839.   **I WISH NOAH HAD SWATTED THOSE TWO MOSQUITOS**

Rating 1 2 3 4 5 Date Used: _____

840.   **ONE CAN'T AVOID GETTING OLDER, BUT LIVING OLD IS A CHOICE**

Rating 1 2 3 4 5 Date Used: _____

841. FAITH CANNOT STAND UNLESS IT BE FOUNDED ON THE PROMISES OF GOD — JOHN CALVIN

Rating 1 2 3 4 5 Date Used: _____

842. THE WORD OF GOD IS PERFECT; IT IS PRECISE AND PURE; IT IS TRUTH ITSELF — MARTIN LUTHER

Rating 1 2 3 4 5 Date Used: _____

843. BIBLICAL ORTHODOXY WITHOUT COMPASSION IS SURELY UGLY — FRANCIS SCHAEFFER

Rating 1 2 3 4 5 Date Used: _____

844. AVIOD DOING WHAT YOU WOULD BLAME OTHERS FOR DOING — THALES

Rating 1 2 3 4 5 Date Used: _____

845. WISDOM IS KNOWING THE RIGHT PATH TO TAKE INTEGRITY IS TAKING IT — M.H. MCKEE

Rating 1 2 3 4 5 Date Used: _____

846. BECAUSE CHRIST AROSE
WE TO SHALL ARISE
LOVE LIFTED US
NOW SAFE ARE WE

Rating 1 2 3 4 5   Date Used: _____

847. THE TRUE MEASURE
OF GOD'S LOVE IS THAT
HE LOVES WITHOUT
MEASURE

Rating 1 2 3 4 5   Date Used: _____

848. PRAYER WITHOUT
THANKSGIVING IS LIKE
A BIRD WITHOUT WINGS
— WM. HENDRICKSEN

Rating 1 2 3 4 5   Date Used: _____

849. DAYS OF TROUBLE MUST
BE DAYS OF PRAYER
— MATTHEW HENRY

Rating 1 2 3 4 5   Date Used: _____

850. WITHIN THE BIBLE ARE
THE ANSWERS FOR ALL
THE PROBLEMS MEN FACE
— RONALD REAGAN

Rating 1 2 3 4 5   Date Used: _____

851. **LOVING THE STATUS QUO ELIMINATES PROGRESS**

Rating 1 2 3 4 5 Date Used: _____

852. **IF PEOPLE TALK BEHIND YOUR BACK. YOU'RE AHEAD OF THEM**

Rating 1 2 3 4 5 Date Used: _____

853. **TRUTH CARRIES A WEIGHT THAT NO LIE CAN COUNTER — JOHN HAGEE**

Rating 1 2 3 4 5 Date Used: _____

854. **A NATION WITHOUT GOD HAS NO HOPE AND BECOMES SATAN'S PLAYGROUND**

Rating 1 2 3 4 5 Date Used: _____

855. **GOD IS MORE WILLING TO GIVE THAN WE ARE TO ASK — ANDREW MURRAY**

Rating 1 2 3 4 5 Date Used: _____

856. WATER AND OIL ARE MORE
COMPATIBLE THAN
CHRISTIANITY & PREDJUDICE
— WILLIAM A. WARD

Rating 1 2 3 4 5 Date Used: _____

857. CHRISTIANITY IS IN ITS
VERY ESSENCE A
RESURRECTION RELIGION
— JOHN R.W. STOTT

Rating 1 2 3 4 5 Date Used: _____

858. WHEN I MET CHRIST
I FELT LIKE I HAD
SWALLOWED SUNSHINE
— E. STANLEY JONES

Rating 1 2 3 4 5 Date Used: _____

859. LOSE MONEY – BAD
LOSE FRIEND – WORSE
LOSE FAITH – LOSE ALL

Rating 1 2 3 4 5 Date Used: _____

860. INSPIRATION DOES
EXIST, BUT IT MUST
FIND YOU WORKING
— PABLO PICASSO

Rating 1 2 3 4 5 Date Used: _____

861. HOPE IS BEING ABLE
TO SEE LIGHT WHEN
ALL IS DARKNESS
— DESMOND TUTU

Rating 1 2 3 4 5 Date Used: _____

862. ONLY LIGHT CAN DRIVE
OUT DARKNESS, ONLY
LOVE CAN DRIVE OUT
HATE – M. L. KING JR.

Rating 1 2 3 4 5 Date Used: _____

863. LOVE IS LIKE THE
WIND, YOU CAN'T SEE
IT BUT YOU CAN FEEL IT
— CATHERINE VALENTE

Rating 1 2 3 4 5 Date Used: _____

864. HAVE A PROBLEM?
GOD IS AVAILABLE
LET HIM DO THE
HEAVY LIFTING

Rating 1 2 3 4 5 Date Used: _____

865. ONE HOUR IN HEAVEN
AND WE'LL BE ASHAMED
WE EVER GRUMBLED
— VANCE HAVNER

Rating 1 2 3 4 5 Date Used: _____

866. ALL TRUE EVANGELISM
IS THEOLOGY IN ACTION
— J. I. PACKER

Rating   1   2   3   4   5   Date Used: _____

867. NEVER MISS A CHANCE TO
SEE SOMETHING BEAUTIFUL
BEAUTY IS GOD'S HANDWRITING
— CHARLES KINGSLEY

Rating   1   2   3   4   5   Date Used: _____

868. DOING SOMETHING FOR
SOMEONE WHO CAN NEVER
REPAY IS TRUE LOVE
IN ACTION

Rating   1   2   3   4   5   Date Used: _____

869. THE DIRECTION OF THE
WIND IS SET BUT WE CAN
SET OUR SAILS TO GET
SAFELY HOME

Rating   1   2   3   4   5   Date Used: _____

870. IF WE FACE THE SONSHINE
THE SHADOWS WILL
ALWAYS BE BEHIND US

Rating   1   2   3   4   5   Date Used: _____

871. THE RESULT OF LIVING IN A SECULAR AGE IS SECULARISM BECOMES THE DEFAULT SETTING

Rating 1 2 3 4 5 Date Used: _____

872. RELIGION IN THE PUBLIC SQUARE IS BECOMING AN ENDANGERED SPECIES
— MATT STAVER

Rating 1 2 3 4 5 Date Used: _____

873. THE SOUL WOULD HAVE NO RAINBOW IF THE EYES HAD NO TEARS
— JOHN VANCE CHENEY

Rating 1 2 3 4 5 Date Used: _____

874. THOSE WHO SOW IN TEARS SHALL REAP IN JOY
— PSALM 126:5

Rating 1 2 3 4 5 Date Used: _____

875. LOOK UNTO JESUS EVEN THROUGH YOUR TEARS
— DR. JOSEPH PARKER

Rating 1 2 3 4 5 Date Used: _____

876. WHEN THE DEVIL STARTS MESS-IN THE LORD STARTS BLESS-IN

Rating 1 2 3 4 5   Date Used: _____

877. HELL IS THE HIGHEST REWARD THE DEVIL CAN OFFER A FOLLOWER
— BILLY SUNDAY

Rating 1 2 3 4 5   Date Used: _____

878. WORSHIP IS NOT ABOUT US IT'S ABOUT HIM
— DAVID JEREMIAH

Rating 1 2 3 4 5   Date Used: _____

879. MAKE FAILURE YOUR TEACHER NOT YOUR UNDERTAKER
— JOHN HAGEE

Rating 1 2 3 4 5   Date Used: _____

880. EDUCATION WITHOUT VALUES SEEMS TO MAKE A CLEVER DEVIL
— C.S. LEWIS

Rating 1 2 3 4 5   Date Used: _____

881. THE LEARNING PROCESS CONTINUES UNTIIL THE DAY YOU DIE — KIRK DOUGLAS

Rating 1 2 3 4 5   Date Used: _____

882. ONE DAY YOUR LIFE WILL FLASH BEFORE YOUR EYES MAKE SURE ITS WORTH WATCHING — G. WAY

Rating 1 2 3 4 5   Date Used: _____

883. NEVER GIVE UP EVEN A SNAIL MADE THE ARK

Rating 1 2 3 4 5   Date Used: _____

884. PEOPLE LIVING IN CHRIST HAVE NO FEAR OF DEATH

Rating 1 2 3 4 5   Date Used: _____

885. THE BEST RUBRICS OF WORSHIP ARE THOSE WRITTEN ON BROKEN HEARTS — C. SPURGEON

Rating 1 2 3 4 5   Date Used: _____

886. OBEDIENCE IS THE END
OF OUR CALLING
— JOHN CALVIN

Rating   1   2   3   4   5   Date Used: _____

887. THE PURER YOUR HABITS
THE CLOSER TO GOD
YOU WILL COME
— RAVI ZACHARIAS

Rating   1   2   3   4   5   Date Used: _____

888. THE WAY TO COVER OUR
SIN IS TO UNCOVER IT
BY CONFESSION
— RICHARD SIBBES

Rating   1   2   3   4   5   Date Used: _____

889. IF YOU THINK EDUCATION
IS EXPENSIVE TRY
IGNORANCE

Rating   1   2   3   4   5   Date Used: _____

890. LIFE IS A VOYAGE
THAT'S HOMEWARD
BOUND
— HERMAN MELVILLE

Rating   1   2   3   4   5   Date Used: _____

891. **LOVE OPENS HEARTS FEAR AND DISTRUST CLOSES THEM**

Rating   1   2   3   4   5   Date Used: _____

892. **HAPPINESS IS LIKE A BOOMERANG - GIVE AND IT COMES BACK**

Rating   1   2   3   4   5   Date Used: _____

893. **THE PLACE WHERE DREAMS GO TO DIE IS CALLED IMPOSSIBILITY**

Rating   1   2   3   4   5   Date Used: _____

894. **CHAMPIONS KEEP ON PLAYING UNTIL THEY GET IT RIGHT — BILLY JEAN KING**

Rating   1   2   3   4   5   Date Used: _____

895. **LITTLE MINDS ARE TAMED BY MISFORTUNE, BUT GREAT MINDS RISE ABOVE IT — WASHINGTON IRVING**

Rating   1   2   3   4   5   Date Used: _____

896. IF YOU WANT LIGHT
IN YOUR LIFE STAND
IN THE SONSHINE

Rating 1 2 3 4 5 Date Used: _____

897. FALURE DEFEATS LOSERS
FALURE MOTIVATES
WINNERS

Rating 1 2 3 4 5 Date Used: _____

898. HOPE NEVER ABANDONS
YOU, YOU ADANDON IT
— GEORGE WEINBERG

Rating 1 2 3 4 5 Date Used: _____

899. ABOVE EVERY STORM
THE SON IS SHINING

Rating 1 2 3 4 5 Date Used: _____

900. LOVE REMOVES MASKS
AND REVEALS TRUTH
MAKING RELATIONSHIPS
WHOLE AND POSITIVE

Rating 1 2 3 4 5 Date Used: _____

901. INEXPENSIVE WAY TO
CHANGE YOUR LOOKS
IS TO SMILE

Rating 1 2 3 4 5 Date Used: _____

902. MAN MADE IN THE IMAGE OF GOD HAS A PURPOSE: TO HAVE A RELATIONSHIP
— FRANCIS SCHAFFER

Rating 1 2 3 4 5 Date Used: _____

903. EVERY CHRISTIAN IS EITHER A MISSIONARY OR AN IMPOSTOR
— CHARLES SPURGEON

Rating 1 2 3 4 5 Date Used: _____

904. TRUE FAITH IS ALWAYS CONNECTED WITH HOPE
— JOHN CALVIN

Rating 1 2 3 4 5 Date Used: _____

905. OUR REPUTATION IS FOR THIS WORLD OUR CHARACTER IS FOR ETERNITY

Rating 1 2 3 4 5 Date Used: _____

906. PREACHING HAS AUTHORITY ONLY WHEN THE MESSAGE IS FROM GOD HIMSELF
— J.I. PACKER

Rating 1 2 3 4 5 Date Used: _____

907. DON'T LET YESTERDAY
TAKE UP TOO MUCH
OF TODAY
— WILL ROGERS

Rating 1 2 3 4 5   Date Used: _____

908. I NEVER LOSE I EITHER
WIN OR LEARN
— NELSON MANDELA

Rating 1 2 3 4 5   Date Used: _____

909. REMEMBER TODAY IS THE
TOMORROW YOU WORRIED
ABOUT YESTERDAY
— DALE CARNEGIE

Rating 1 2 3 4 5   Date Used: _____

910. ALWAYS FORGIVE YOUR
ENEMIES – NOTHING
ANNOYS THEM MORE
— OSCAR WILDE

Rating 1 2 3 4 5   Date Used: _____

911. THE SUN IS NO LESS
BRIGHT BECAUSE BLIND
MEN DON'T PERCIEVE IT
— JOHN CALVIN

Rating 1 2 3 4 5   Date Used: _____

**912. SALVATION WITHOUT
        DISCIPLESHIP IS
        CHEAP GRACE
        — DIETRICH BONHOFFER**

Rating 1 2 3 4 5   Date Used: _____

**913. GOOD WORKS ARE
        ARE WORTH MUCH
        AND COST LITTLE
        — GEORGE HERBERT**

Rating 1 2 3 4 5   Date Used: _____

**914. THERE IS NO JOY IN THE
        WORLD LIKE THR JOY OF
        BRINGING ONE SOUL TO
        CHRIST — WM. BARCLAY**

Rating 1 2 3 4 5   Date Used: _____

**915. MARRIAGE WAS CONCEIVE
        AND BORN IN GOD'S MIND
        — MAX LUCADO**

Rating 1 2 3 4 5   Date Used: _____

**916. THE GLORY OF
        CHRISTIANITY IS TO
        CONQUER BY FORGIVENESS
        — WILLIAM BLAKE**

Rating 1 2 3 4 5   Date Used: _____

917. TRUTHFULNESS IS A SOIL IN WHICH PRIDE DOES NOT EASILY GROW — MICHAEL RAMSEY

Rating 1 2 3 4 5 Date Used: _____

918. LOVE IS NOT VALIDATED WITH WORDS BUT BY ACTIONS

Rating 1 2 3 4 5 Date Used: _____

919. VICTIMS HURT MORE FROM THE SILENCE OF THE BYSTANDER THEN THE CRUELTY OF THE OPPRESSOR – ELIE WIESEL

Rating 1 2 3 4 5 Date Used: _____

920. HOLOCAUST DENIAL IS NOT JUST IGNORANCE IT IS MODERN ANTI-SEMITISM

Rating 1 2 3 4 5 Date Used: _____

921. GOD IS THE GREATEST PROMISE KEEPER

Rating 1 2 3 4 5 Date Used: _____

922. GO OUT ON A LIMB
THAT'S WHERE THE
JUICIEST FRUIT IS
— WILL ROGERS

Rating 1 2 3 4 5 Date Used: _____

923. YOU CAN'T ENSLAVE
A BIBLE BELIEVING
PEOPLE
— HORACE GREELEY

Rating 1 2 3 4 5 Date Used: _____

924. DID GOD SAY REMODEL
THE CHAPEL OR
REFORM THE CHURCH?
— ST. FRANCIS OF ASSISI

Rating 1 2 3 4 5 Date Used: _____

925. NOTHING MORE ENHANCES
AUTHORITY THAN SILENCE
— CHARLES de GAULLE

Rating 1 2 3 4 5 Date Used: _____

926. WE MUST EXPECT FINITE
DISAPPOINTMENT BUT
NEVER LOSE INFINITE HOPE
— MARTIN L. KING JR.

Rating 1 2 3 4 5 Date Used: _____

927.   WHEN THE POWER OF LOVE REPLACES THE LOVE OF POWER WE WILL HAVE PEACE

Rating 1 2 3 4 5 Date Used: _____

928.   YOU CANNOT HAVE A FREE SOCIETY IF THE AIM IS EQUALITY FOR ALL

Rating 1 2 3 4 5 Date Used: _____

929.   THOSE WHO PUT EQUALITY BEFORE LIBERTY ARE NOT LIKELY TO HAVE EITHER — MILTON FRIEDMAN

Rating 1 2 3 4 5 Date Used: _____

930.   EVERYTHING YOU'VE EVER WANTED IS ON THE OTHER SIDE OF FEAR — GEORGE ADAIR

Rating 1 2 3 4 5 Date Used: _____

931.   AS LIGHT DRIVES OUT DARKNESS SO LOVE CAN DRIVE OUT HATE

Rating 1 2 3 4 5 Date Used: _____

932. TO GIVE LESS THAN
ONES BEST IS TO
SACRIFICE ONES
GOD GIVEN GIFTS

Rating 1 2 3 4 5 Date Used: _____

933. BRAVERY IS BEING THE
THE ONLY ONE WHO
KNOWS YOU'RE AFRAID

Rating 1 2 3 4 5 Date Used: _____

934. CONSCIENCE GETS A
LOT OF CREDIT THAT
BELONGS TO COLD FEET

Rating 1 2 3 4 5 Date Used: _____

935. FAITH ALLOWS US TO TURN
OUR INFIRMATIES INTO
DISPLAYS OF HIS GRACE
— CHARLES H. SPURGEON

Rating 1 2 3 4 5 Date Used: _____

936. THE DEVIL IS NOT
AFRAID OF A BIBLE
THAT HAS DUST ON IT

Rating 1 2 3 4 5 Date Used: _____

937. FRUIT IS EVIDENCE
OF THE ROOT
— JOHN BLANCHARD

Rating   1   2   3   4   5   Date Used: _____

938. IF YOU WALK WITH
GOD YOU WILL ALWAYS
BE ON THE RIGHT PATH

Rating   1   2   3   4   5   Date Used: _____

939. LIFE IS HARD – BUT
GOD IS GOOD, AND
HEAVEN IS REAL
— BILLY GRAHAM

Rating   1   2   3   4   5   Date Used: _____

940. IT'S FAR BETTER TO
SEE A SERMON THAN
HEAR ONE

Rating   1   2   3   4   5   Date Used: _____

941. A LIE CAN'T BE A TRUTH
WRONG CAN'T BE RIGHT
EVIL CAN'T BECOME GOOD
BECAUSE A MAJORITY SAY SO

Rating   1   2   3   4   5   Date Used: _____

942. IF EQUAL AFFECTIONS
CANNOT BE
THEN LET THE MOST
LOVING ONE BE ME

Rating 1 2 3 4 5 Date Used: _____

943. A PERSON WRAPPED UP
IN HIMSELF MAKES A
VERY SMALL BUNDLE
— BENJAMIN FRANKLIN

Rating 1 2 3 4 5 Date Used: _____

944. GOD'S PURPOSES
ALWAYS HAVE GOD'S
PROVISION
— JOHN BLANCHARD

Rating 1 2 3 4 5 Date Used: _____

945. IT'S A WEAK FAITH
THAT ONLY SERVES
GOD IN TIMES OF
BLESSING — J. STEDMAN

Rating 1 2 3 4 5 Date Used: _____

946. UNTIL YOU ARE FREE
TO DIE YOU ARE NOT
FREE TO LIVE

Rating 1 2 3 4 5 Date Used: _____

947. THE GOSPEL IS NOT A DOCTRINE OF THE TONGUE BUT OF LIFE — JOHN CALVIN

Rating 1 2 3 4 5   Date Used: _____

948. THE WORLD CREATES TROUBLE IN PEACE GOD CREATES PEACE IN TROUBLE— T. WATSON

Rating 1 2 3 4 5   Date Used: _____

949. WHEN MORALITY IS STRONG LAWS NEED NOT BE

Rating 1 2 3 4 5   Date Used: _____

950. WITHOUT RELIGION THERE CAN BE NO TRUE MORALITY

Rating 1 2 3 4 5   Date Used: _____

951 BECOME A CHILD OF THE KING THE INHERITANCE IS OUT OF THIS WORLD

Rating 1 2 3 4 5   Date Used: _____

952 A CHRISTIAN WITHOUT
A CHURCH IS LIKE AN
ATHLETE WITHOUT
A TEAM

Rating 1 2 3 4 5 Date Used: _____

953. PRAYER IS LETTING
THE MASTER MECHANIC
DO THE REPAIRS

Rating 1 2 3 4 5 Date Used: _____

954. THOSE WHO LIVE RIGHT
WON'T BE LEFT BEHIND

Rating 1 2 3 4 5 Date Used: _____

955. THOSE WHO LIVE IN
GLASS HOUSES
SHOULDN'T GET
STONED

Rating 1 2 3 4 5 Date Used: _____

956. A GOOD RACEHORSE
DOESN'T ASK FOR A
DRY TRACK

Rating 1 2 3 4 5 Date Used: _____

957. A HUMBLE PERSON
NEVER BLOWS THEIR
"KNOWS" IN PUBLIC

Rating 1 2 3 4 5 Date Used: _____

958.   **LAZINESS AND BOREDOM ARE SATAN'S BEST FRIENDS**

Rating 1 2 3 4 5   Date Used: _____

959.   **IF YOU ARE TRULY LIKE JESUS THE WORLD WILL HATE YOU**

Rating 1 2 3 4 5   Date Used: _____

960.   **A BEAUTIFUL HEART TRANSFORMS THE HOMELIEST FACE**

Rating 1 2 3 4 5   Date Used: _____

961.   **GIVING IS A THERMOMETER OF OUR LOVE**

Rating 1 2 3 4 5   Date Used: _____

962.   **A WIFE WHO NAGS TOO MUCH MAY CAUSE HER HUSBAND TO HORSE AROUND**

Rating 1 2 3 4 5   Date Used: _____

963. CIRCUMSTANCES RULE THE WEAK BUT THEY MOTIVATE THE WISE

Rating   1   2   3   4   5   Date Used: _____

964. DON'T MARRY FOR MONEY IT'S EASIER TO BORROW IT

Rating   1   2   3   4   5   Date Used: _____

965. MONEY WILL BUY HAPPINESS ONLY IF YOU SPEND IT ON SOMEONE ELSE

Rating   1   2   3   4   5   Date Used: _____

966. A COMMUNITY OR NATION CAN BE NO STRONGER THAN IT'S MOTHERS AND FAMILIES

Rating   1   2   3   4   5   Date Used: _____

967. GREAT PREACHING REQUIRES GREAT LISTENING

Rating   1   2   3   4   5   Date Used: _____

968.   **THE END NEVER JUSTIFIES MEANESS**

Rating 1 2 3 4 5 Date Used: _____

969.   **PREJUDICE IS THE CHILD OF IGNORANCE**

Rating 1 2 3 4 5 Date Used: _____

970.   **SWALLOW YOUR PRIDE IT'S NOT FATTENING**

Rating 1 2 3 4 5 Date Used: _____

971.   **PROFANITY IS THE USE OF STRONG WORDS BY WEAK PEOPLE**

Rating 1 2 3 4 5 Date Used: _____

972.   **A RELIGION THAT COSTS NOTHING IS WORTH NOTHING**

Rating 1 2 3 4 5 Date Used: _____

973.   **GOD'S PART WE CANNOT DO – OUR PART GOD WILL NOT DO**

Rating 1 2 3 4 5 Date Used: _____

974. **EVERY GENERATION NEEDS A REGENERATION**

Rating 1 2 3 4 5   Date Used: _____

975. **ENVY PROVIDES THE MUD FAILURE THROWS AT SUCCESS**

Rating 1 2 3 4 5   Date Used: _____

976. **GOD TENDS TO USE THE ONE CLOSEST TO HIM**

Rating 1 2 3 4 5   Date Used: _____

977. **YOU CAN'T BECOME DIZZY DOING GOOD TURNS**

Rating 1 2 3 4 5   Date Used: _____

978. **TO SIN IS HUMAN TO CONTINUE IT IS IDIOCY**

Rating 1 2 3 4 5   Date Used: _____

979. **MAKING SIN LEGAL DOES NOT MAKE IT HARMLESS**

Rating 1 2 3 4 5   Date Used: _____

980. SATAN'S MESSAGE
SIN NOW- PAY LATER

Rating 1 2 3 4 5 Date Used: _____

981. A SMILE ADDS
FACE VALUE

Rating 1 2 3 4 5 Date Used: _____

982. OBSTINATE PEOPLE
DON'T HOLD OPINIONS
THEIR OPINIONS
HOLD THEM

Rating 1 2 3 4 5 Date Used: _____

983. ALCOHOL KILLS THE
LIVING AND PRESERVES
THE DEAD

Rating 1 2 3 4 5 Date Used: _____

984. THE ONE THING
CHRISTIANITY CANNOT
BE IS MODERATELY
IMPORTANT — C.S. LEWIS

Rating 1 2 3 4 5 Date Used: _____

985. THANKSGIVING IS GOOD
"THANKSLIVING"
IS BETTER

Rating 1 2 3 4 5 Date Used: _____

986. MOST JOBS ARE BEST DONE BY COMMITTEES OF ONE

Rating 1 2 3 4 5 Date Used: _____

987. LIFE LIVED IN WORRY INVITES DEATH IN A HURRAY

Rating 1 2 3 4 5 Date Used: _____

988. EMOTION WITHOUT DEVOTION IS COMMOTION

Rating 1 2 3 4 5 Date Used: _____

989. TO STAY YOUTHFUL STAY USEFUL

Rating 1 2 3 4 5 Date Used: _____

990. IT'S NEITHER SAFE NOR PRUDENT TO DO ANYTHING AGAINST ONE'S CONSCIENCE — M. LUTHER

Rating 1 2 3 4 5 Date Used: _____

991. ALWAYS STAND ON PRINCIPLE EVEN IF YOU STAND ALONE — JOHN ARAMS

Rating 1 2 3 4 5 Date Used: _____

992. **TROUBLE HEARING GOD'S WORD? PROBLEM MAY BE IN THE RECEIVER**

Rating 1 2 3 4 5 Date Used: _____

993. **LACK OF MORAL CLARITY IS DAMAGING TO NATIONS AND INDIVIDUALS**

Rating 1 2 3 4 5 Date Used: _____

994. **JESUS IS GOD'S DYNAMITE**

Rating 1 2 3 4 5 Date Used: _____

995. **A CHRISTIAN KEEPS PROMISES TO THOSE WHO CANNOT ENFORCE THEM**

Rating 1 2 3 4 5 Date Used: _____

996. **GOD IS MORE INTERESTED IN OUR LOVE THAN IN OUR THEOLOGY**

Rating 1 2 3 4 5 Date Used: _____

997. **SECURITY IN GOD COMES FROM KNOWING THERE IS NO SECURITY IN ANYTHING ELSE**

Rating 1 2 3 4 5 Date Used: _____

998. CHRISTIANITY IS A RELIGION OF TRUST WITH AN ETHICS OF LOVE
— BARTHOLD NEIBHUR

Rating 1 2 3 4 5 Date Used: _____

999. SUCCESS IN LIFE IS MEASURED NOT BY WHAT WE GET BUT BY WHAT WE GIVE

Rating 1 2 3 4 5 Date Used: _____

1000. MISTAKES ARE NORMAL ENCORES ARE NOT

Rating 1 2 3 4 5 Date Used: _____

1001. PEOPLE ARE LIKE THE MOON THEY CAN'T SHINE WITHOUT THE SON

Rating 1 2 3 4 5 Date Used: _____

About the Author

Dr. L. James Harvey was born and raised in Grand Rapids Michigan. He is an honor graduate of Hope College and has MA and PhD degrees from Michigan State University. Dr. Harvey has been a high school teacher and coach, a college dean, vice president, and president, and a senior vice-president and partner in an international management consulting firm in based in Washington D.C.

Dr. Harvey has had wide experience in speaking, consulting, teaching, and leading workshops, and seminars in the U.S. and overseas. Speaking largely to college and university faculties and staffs, he gained national recognition as a speaker and consultant in the area of college and university management. He also published three books and several articles in his area of expertise.

Dr. Harvey, and his wife of 68 years, have been active Christian laypersons wherever they have lived. Both are ordained elders, Sunday school teachers, and have held leadership positions in churches in two denominations, the

Reformed Church in America, and the Moravian Church in America. Dr. Harvey has also served as a trustee on the boards of seminaries in both denominations. Since Dr. Harvey stopped working for a living (retirement will never be an option) he has begun speaking and writing on topics related to successful aging and the Christian life. He has now published ten books, two of which are co-authored with Jackie.

In recent years Dr. Harvey and his wife have returned to Grand Rapids, Michigan for their encore years where both were born and raised.

Other book titles are listed below and/or can be seen on Dr. Harvey's web site at: **www.sentencesermons.com**

Other Book Titles From Dr. Harvey

1. *701 Sentence Sermons*. (Grand Rapids, Michigan: Kregel Publications, 2000)

2. *701 More Sentence Sermons*. (Grand Rapids, Michigan: Kregel Publications, 2002)

3 *701 Sentence Sermons* – Vol. 3 (Grand Rapids, Michigan: Kregel

Publications, 2005)

4. *701 Sentence Sermons* – Vol. 4 (Grand Rapids, Michigan: Kregel Publications, 2007)

5. *Every Day is Saturday* (with Jackie Harvey). (St. Louis, Missouri: Concordia Publishing House, 2000) (Limited availability)

6. *The Resurrection – Ruse or Reality?* (Rapid City, South Dakota: CrossLink Publishing, 2011)

7. *Letters from Perverse University*. (Lincoln, Nebraska: Author's Press, 2001)

8. *Seven for Heaven*. (Lima, Ohio: CSS Publishing Co., 2003)

9. *Run Thru the Tape*. (Rapid City, South Dakota: CrossLink Publishing, 2009)

10. *Does God Laugh?* (Traverse City, Michigan: Harvest Day Books, 2008)

CPSIA information can be obtained
at www.ICGtesting.com
Printed in the USA
FSHW021121080521
81173FS

9 781637 693261